Lordship Salvation:

The *Only* Kind There Is

An evaluation of Jody Dillow's *The Reign of Servant Kings* and other antinomian arguments

by Curtis I. Crenshaw

Lordship Salvation: The Only Kind There Is

© Footstool Publications 1994
PO Box 161021
Memphis, TN 38186

ISBN: 1-877818-12-7

To my wonderful daughter, Chandra

You are my precious flower, given to me by Almighty God to cherish, nourish, love, train in righteousness, and protect until I give you to some other man to continue what I have begun. May the Lordship of Jesus always guide you in the truth of His infallible Word.

Table of Contents

Foreword

by Dr. John H. Gerstner

From what I have read of Jody Dillow's *The Reign of Servant Kings*, it is a significant effort to defend classical Dispensationalism. In spite of MacArthur's *The Gospel According to Jesus*, of Crenshaw and Gunn's *Dispensationalism Today, Yesterday, and Tomorrow*, of Ken Gentry's *Lord of the Saved*, of Poythress' *Understanding Dispensationalism*, and my own *Wrongly Dividing the Word of Truth* (soon to be followed by *Wrongly Dividing Wrongly Dividing*), plus other lesser known works, I have not seen much substantive reply by Dispensationalists. Charles Ryrie, John Witmer and the President of Master's Seminary have rejected these attacks with vigor but for the most part by merely re-asserting their Dispensational orthodoxy.

Jody Dillow has made an impressive effort really to defend Dispensationalism and thoroughly refute its contemporary critics. I think that Curtis Crenshaw shows in this book that Dillow's mighty efforts are futile. The sheer length and relative profundity of Dillow makes this rebuttal all the more important if for no other reason than its demonstrating that the best endeavors to revive Dispensationalism are trying to blow life into a corpse (which Gary North and Ken Gentry have been saying for some time).

Though Crenshaw may be guilty of over beating a dead horse, the sad fact is that this one will not die easily. Our author has waited nearly a decade for his (and Gunn's) book to be noticed. So this Dillow refutation rather understandably abounds in "Dillow has typically misquoted him" and "Dillow has typically either misunderstood or misrepresented." I can only join Crenshaw in hoping (probably another vain hope) that Jody Dillow will see that he deserves most of the lovingly-administered epithets!

Acknowledgments

Jay Green is the one who sent me Dillow's book to read, asking that I do a review of it. I had been wanting to write something on the lordship issue for many years, and this gave me the excuse I needed. My thanks to Jay Green for asking me to do so and then printing much of the book in his publication.

Thomas M. "Pete" Frye and I attended seminary together, having fought many of the same theological battles. He read the manuscript for its theology, and his insights have been incorporated.

David Potts is an extraordinary man, having taught *himself* how to use computers and graphics software. He configures his own systems, repairs them, installs his own software, and does just about anything ---- all without having a single course in school. He usually does our book covers, and this one is no exception.

On a Friday afternoon, I gave this manuscript to Teresa Johnson and asked her to edit it quickly. The following Saturday, early in the afternoon, she called. I thought she had a question for me, but instead she announced that she was done! Few people could do a job well and quickly, but this college English professor with a master's degree has done so. Any mistakes remaining are strictly mine, probably because I did not take her advice.

Thanks also to James E. Rosscup, professor at the Master's Seminary, for encouraging us to put this in print.

Introduction

I was in seminary with Jody Dillow though we did not know one another well, only casually. Jody was several years ahead of me and did his doctorate at our seminary, Dallas Theological Seminary (hereafter DTS). I was graduated in 1976 with a Th. M.

Not long after I entered DTS, I came into the Reformed faith. While sick at home with the flu and a kidney stone, I read Warfield's *Perfectionism*, Van Til's *Defense of the Faith*, and Luther's *Bondage of the Will*, which completely changed me. From this point forward, I fought continual battles in seminary over the lordship issue and the carnal Christian theory.

It is a shame that there are so many battles over something so simple as the Gospel, but some adherents to dispensationalism, especially those associated with DTS, have challenged the old Gospel. While denying the nature of regeneration and faith/repentance, disconnecting the relationship between faith and works, and making personal assurance part of the Gospel, they have become antinomians. All this springs from their denial of the sovereignty of God, from their so-called literal hermeneutic, and from their misunderstanding of the Reformed, whom they wrongly accuse of teaching a works salvation.

My goals in this evaluation of anti-lordship salvation are several: to demonstrate Dillow's (and anti-lordship advocates in general) logical inconsistencies, to show his faulty hermeneutic (method of interpretation), his theological errors, his exegetical atrocities, and to present the truth in contradiction to his heresies.

The present book is an expansion of a series of articles I did in the *Herald of the Covenant* about eight years ago, and each chapter now (except chapter 5) was an article then.

Most of the biblical quotes are from the New King James Version.

1

The Heresy & Its Causes

This chapter considers the nature of the error and other considerations to help us analyze Dillow's weaknesses discussed in the chapters that follow.

Discerning Dillow's Heresy

The Issue

In 1989 John MacArthur wrote a book entitled *The Gospel According to Jesus,* in which he demonstrated from the Gospels that Jesus taught lordship salvation. MacArthur is a dispensationalist, making his book especially stinging to other dispensationalists. Quickly Charles Ryrie responded with *So Great Salvation* and Zane Hodges with *Absolutely Free!* Ryrie had been the head of the theology department and Hodges head of the New Testament department, both at DTS. Jody Dillow has now written a very detailed book (1992) entitled *The Reign of the Servant Kings* in which he espouses the no lordship view.

Dillow's book attempts to be scholarly in answering John MacArthur's work while Ryrie and Hodges have made a more popular effort to do so. Dillow's work is neither scholarly nor comes close to overturning MacArthur's work. If one considers scholarship to be numerous footnotes and mountains of research, then Dillow's work qualifies. If, however, scholarship is delving into the essence of an argument with great insight and refuting that argument, then Dillow has failed.[1]

---

[1]There is nothing new in Dillow's book that I did not hear for four years in

The issue, therefore, is antinomianism, the idea that good works are not a *necessary* part of salvation. We must avoid two heresies: that works are a condition to obtain justification, the forgiveness of sins and the gift of Christ's righteousness (legalism), and that works are not a necessary fruit of our justification (antinomianism).[2]

When we say works are a necessary part of salvation, we do not mean they are a condition for justification (avoiding legalism) but the fruit of sanctification (avoiding license). If grace is free or irresistible, if regeneration gives a person the desire and ability to please God, if faith cannot exist unless it works, if sanctification necessarily is the effect of justification, if assurance of personal faith must have fruit and is not of the essence of faith, then perseverance in faith and holiness with works as the necessary fruit is the inevitable conclusion. One could not embrace Christ as Savior without embracing Him as Lord.

Antinomians have various ways of expressing their view: one can know Christ as Savior and not as Lord; there are three kinds of people in the world: non-Christians, spiritual Christians who have *allowed* Jesus to be their Lord, and carnal Christians who have not allowed Jesus to be their Lord; the one justified does not necessarily persevere in faith and holiness; in the new birth we have a new nature imparted to the Christian so that the Christian has two natures; only godly Christians abide in Christ while carnal Christians do not abide in Him; one must believe in Christ to keep from going to hell and *optionally* be a disciple of Christ to gain rewards; assurance of salvation has nothing to do with God's working to conform a believer to Christ so that if one thinks he is justified, he is; one must believe in Christ but repentance is not required; and many other such things. But in each state-

---

seminary. I have read every book the "carnal Christian" men have written, studied under their best theologians, evaluated their most detailed arguments, dialogued with them in person, debated fellow students and pastors for over twenty years, and they all essentially say the same.

[2]Though the brand of antinomianism we are discussing is primarily in dispensationalism, it is possible to be antinomian and not dispensational. Consequently I have placed the discussion of antinomianism in dispensationalism in appendix 3.

ment works are not a *necessary* result of conversion.

The Danger

I have often warned pastors that with this license theology they would confirm church members to hell by giving them a false assurance, telling them they are Christians even though they have no change in their lives. This rank theology is defended in Dillow's book. We are not debating minor issues in the Bible; we are at the heart of the Gospel of grace. Ryrie noted this long ago in *Balancing the Christian Life* when he stated that Reformed writers A. W. Pink and J. I. Packer were preaching a false Gospel (p. 169) because they believed that Jesus must be Lord to be Savior. I agree with Ryrie that both views cannot be the Gospel.

Because Dillow (and Zane Hodges) is closer to orthodoxy than Jehovah's Witnesses, he is more dangerous. I'm afraid many will be in hell who thought they had embraced Jesus but were only comfortable with a false faith. Just as legalism or earning one's justification is not the Gospel and we rightly classify those who preach such as heretics (Gal. 1:8, 9), so also license or dead faith is not the Gospel (James 2:14ff; 1 John 2:3, 4). The license view is simply the other side of the coin to legalism; if one is heresy so is the other.

The History

The license position was first promoted in dispensationalism by Lewis Sperry Chafer, the founder of DTS, then by John Walvoord, and in turn by J. Dwight Pentecost and Charles C. Ryrie. Zane Hodges, a later generation than these men, was the most radical and the most consistent with this view, from whom, no doubt, Dillow learned the optional holiness view, as he uses the same passages and arguments as Hodges. Chafer studied at Oberlin, the school founded by the virtually pure Pelagians, Asa Mahan and Charles Finney. Though Chafer did not adopt pure Pelagianism, he adopted its assumption: the autonomy of man, especially in conversion. If W. H. Griffith Thomas had lived to teach theology at DTS, I doubt that the lordship controversy would have occurred.[3]

---

[3]For example, see his comments on faith and works in *The Principles of Theology* (London: Vine Books Ltd, 1978), p. 200ff.

While I was a student at DTS, many of the professors, however, did not hold to this radical view, among whom were S. Lewis Johnson, Ed Blum, John Hannah, Phil Williams and others. They held to perseverance.

Dillow has departed even from what at DTS would be considered orthodoxy and what other dispensational institutions would consider true theology. Indeed, Zane Hodges was viewed by many other DTS professors as not even in the tradition of Chafer, Walvoord, Ryrie, and as having gone far beyond their views. For example, Chafer, Walvoord, and Ryrie would say that one must manifest some sanctification in his life or he is not a Christian, but Hodges denies this. According to Hodges and now Dillow, one can even be an unbeliever and still be a Christian! This view is not shared by the former three professors. Therefore, though Chafer, Walvoord, and Ryrie held the same basic presuppositions as Hodges and Dillow, they did not become as radical, which has required them (Hodges and Dillow) to reinterpret virtually the whole New Testament in terms not shared by any Protestant since the Reformation. Even though Ryrie endorses the book, I truly doubt that he has grasped the implications of what Dillow is saying: One can engage in cannibalism, murder his children, blaspheme God, deny the Trinity, have a dead faith, rape, deny Jesus, never darken the door of a church, be a constant liar, promote abortion and thereby be a murderer, and yet because he has mouthed the name of Jesus, he is considered a Christian. If there is any "theology" more despicable than this and given more to license, I don't know what it is.

The Solution

The Reformed men do not think that one can lose his justification because God causes His saints to persevere in faith and holiness, but at least we would agree with Arminians that personal holiness is not optional in the Christian's life. *We emphasize again that this doctrine of optional holiness in the Christian life is rank heresy, promoting a faith that has no works, and is as much a departure from the Gospel as the doctrine of justification by our works.*

The Reformed position maintains the purity of the Gospel against both legalism and license. Against legalism, we maintain that sinners are justified by faith alone in Christ alone, and against license we believe that the kind of faith that justifies is not alone, but "ever accompanied by good works" (Westminster Confession of Faith, hereafter WCF). Against legalism grace gives us faith, and against license the same grace enables us to persevere. Against legalism eternal life is a free gift and against license new life necessarily manifests itself in the believer. If man's will merits grace, we have legalism, God being indebted to us. If the reception of God's grace does not produce a necessary change in one's life, we have a license to sin. If grace necessarily produces our response, we have balance: eternal life as a free gift in answer to a faith produced by grace and a faith that works.

Maintaining Biblical Balance

Heresy is often truth out of balance, and this is certainly true with Dillow. He holds to many biblical truths, such as the new birth, justification by faith in Christ, and assurance of salvation, but he does not maintain the complete biblical truth on any of these.

Dillow's Position Is Out of Balance

Dillow has Charles Ryrie's approval as seen in his recommendation on the back cover:

> In this penetrating critique of Westminster Calvinism, Dr. Dillow has given us a comprehensive discussion of eternal security and rewards. By a constant appeal to scripture, the biblical doctrine of eternal security is supported instead of the Reformed doctrine of perseverance.

Earl Radmacher, who wrote the introduction to the book, says that now at last, since the controversy between Arminians and Calvinists at the Synod of Dort in 1619, we have a mediating position, a solution to the problem of Arminianism versus Calvinism. These men are delighted that now the Calvinistic Reformed view is challenged systematically at every point and — in their minds — laid to rest. This is incredible naivete.

At least now perhaps the DTS men who follow Dillow will

stop claiming to be Calvinists or Reformed. The men who endorse the book think that Dillow has successfully challenged Westminster Calvinism, which obviously places them outside the Reformed Faith. Now that they have definitely made the break with traditional Calvinism, I hope it is permanent (unless they repent and embrace the Reformed Faith totally). They also deny that they are Arminian, not realizing that their assumptions reveal that they are Arminian.

The reason there can be no harmony between Arminianism and Calvinism nor a moderating position is that they are exact opposites, and the reason there can be no third solution is because there are precisely only two possibilities: Either man works because God irresistibly enables him to do so, or else God works because man lets Him. Grace engages human works or human works engage grace. For 650 pages Dillow does not show any understanding of this simple dilemma, though his constant assumption is that our works engage God's works. He maintains that if we do not *allow* God to sanctify us, then it will not happen; but if God's grace is a pure gift, not earned in any sense, then it has to be irresistible. Dillow wants to maintain that grace is free, but then he also wants the believer to earn his grace for perseverance. He is oblivious to this contradiction.

> Not only had she given her life to Christ, but she had also *allowed* Christ to be formed in her [emphasis added] (p. 61).

> But growth is not automatic; it is conditioned upon our responses (p. 136).

> While justification is based on faith alone and is a work of God, sanctification is uniformly presented in Scripture as a work of man and God (Phil. 2:12-13) and is achieved by faith plus works (p. 147).

This last quote shows how seriously Dillow misunderstands the Bible, for Paul states that the reason we work in our sanctification is because God is enabling us to do so. It may be that Dillow thinks he believes in irresistible grace for justification, but he clearly holds to resistible grace for sanctification.

Any gospel which breaks a man from sin's power and gives

him new life and *motivation* not to sin is not subject to the charge that it logically results in license, *even if an individual Christian resists the positive influences of grace* [emphasis added] (p. 184).

But if Dillow is not Reformed, he is Arminian. He teaches that grace for sanctification is only an influence, a "motivation," or moral persuasion, which is emphatically Arminian, making God only able to persuade the man to persevere, leaving the sinner sovereign over God. How Dillow reconciles that sin's power is broken but still rules the Christian is a mystery. According to Dillow, sin's power is manifested in a disobedient will, which will has been subdued by grace, except when it "resists positive influences," which means it has not been subdued.

As John Gerstner has shown in his excellent book against dispensationalism, *Wrongly Dividing the Word of Truth*, it is not the Reformed position to claim to believe in total depravity while maintaining "free will," to assert belief in election while denying reprobation, to promote the Lord's substitutionary death while proclaiming that some for whom He substituted do not go free, to lay claim to irresistible grace while maintaining God regenerates only when the sinner is ready and that regeneration is by faith, and to proclaim eternal security without also holding to perseverance. At each point Dillow takes back with one hand what he had given with the other, and at each point he reveals his true beliefs.[4]

This confusion regarding the Reformed faith is palpable all through Dillow's work. One example comes to mind: ". . . a person could hold the view that repentance means 'turning from sin' and is a necessary ingredient of saving faith and still deny the Reformed doctrine of perseverance" (p. 30).[5] He does not explain how such a thing is possible, for how can one say that saving faith *necessarily* implies turning from sin and yet the person who has this saving faith may not turn from sin his whole Christian life?

---

[4]The reader is strongly urged to read Gerstner's book, *Wrongly Dividing the Word of Truth* (Brentwood, TN: Wolgemuth & Hyatt, 1991) if he can find a copy, especially chs. 11-13 on antinomianism. The publisher has gone out of business.

[5]Unless otherwise stated, page numbers in parentheses refer to Dillow's book.

This is not, however, the normal position of Arminians, for they at least do not teach that one can practice disobedience and still be a Christian. According to them, the Christian who did so would lose his salvation, which avoids license.[6] Dillow's imbalance, therefore, is that he holds to Arminianism, to resistible grace and consequently that holiness is optional in the Christian's life, being allowed or disallowed as he chooses. Since the Christian cannot lose his justification, he has the license to sin.

The Reformed Position Is Balanced

The Calvinist position is decidedly not eternal security without the other side of the coin, which is perseverance. Dillow and the others must not call themselves Calvinists, for at the Synod of Dort in 1619 the Calvinist position was fossilized to include at least the five points: TULIP. Anything less than this is not Calvinism as historically defined. Anyone who reads the Fifth Head of Doctrine from Dort knows that perseverance is what they taught. They did not teach, however, that a saint will not sin. This seems to be Dillow's understanding of the Reformed doctrine of perseverance. Nothing could be further from the truth. Dort explains that saints do sin:

> Although the weakness of the flesh cannot prevail against the power of God [Dillow thinks God cannot prevail against our flesh unless we *let* Him], who confirms and preserves true believers in a state of grace, yet converts are not always so influenced and actuated by the Spirit of God as not in some particular instances sinfully to deviate from the guidance of divine grace, so as to be seduced by and to comply with the lusts of the flesh. . . . (Article 3).

This does not deny perseverance, and the rest of the many articles under this Fifth Head promote perseverance in faith and holiness. The root error, as we have observed, is that Dillow and others do not believe in irresistible grace, maintaining that man by his will decides whether he will persevere or not. In other words, perseverance depends on the will of man, albeit a regenerate man to choose whether to persevere.

---

[6]This comes close to the legalistic problem, though, for it appears that Arminians teach that Christians must earn their salvation.

It is left to him.[7]

Again this grossly misses the point. A regenerate man has been changed so thoroughly that he now *wants* to please God, and furthermore the Holy Spirit continually maintains him in his perseverance. It is a contradiction of the highest order to believe that one can be regenerated (born again) and still have the same old desires. He has been renewed, old things have passed away and all things have become new (2 Cor. 5:17). Notice what Dort said:

> The Synod rejects the errors of those who teach: that God does indeed provide the believer with sufficient powers to persevere, and is ever ready to preserve these in him if he will do his duty; but that, though all things which are necessary to persevere in faith and which God will use to preserve faith are made use of, even then it ever depends on the pleasure of the will whether it will persevere or not.

> For this contains an outspoken Pelagianism, and while it would make men free, it makes them robbers of God's honor, contrary to the prevailing agreement of the evangelical doctrine, which takes from man all cause of boasting, and ascribes all the praise for this favor to the grace of God alone. . . .

Observe how clear and balanced the WCF is:

> **CONCERNING SANCTIFICATION**: They, who are at once effectually called, and regenerated, having a new heart, and a new spirit created in them, are further sanctified, really and personally [Ed: not just "positionally"], through the virtue of Christ's death and resurrection, by His Word and Spirit dwelling in them: the dominion of the whole body is destroyed, and the several lusts thereof are more and more weakened and mortified ["old nature" or indwelling sin is destroyed]; and they more and more quickened and strengthened in all saving graces, to the practice of true holiness, without which no man shall see the Lord (Chapter 13).

> **CONCERNING SAVING FAITH**: But the principal acts of saving faith are accepting, receiving, and resting upon Christ alone for justification, sanctification, and eternal life. . .

---

[7]This is not even semi-semi-Pelagianism, as Warfield describes it in *The Plan of Salvation*, but semi-Pelagianism.

(Chapter 14)

CONCERNING GOOD WORKS: These good works, done in obedience to God's commandments, are the fruits and evidences of a true and lively faith. . . . Their [saints] ability to do good works is not at all of themselves, but wholly from the Spirit of Christ [works stem from grace, not the reverse]. And that they may be enabled thereunto, beside the graces they have already received, there is required an actual influence [not moral persuasion as the Pelagians teach, for note the rest of the words] of the same Holy Spirit, to work in them to will, and to do, of His good pleasure: yet are they not hereupon to grow negligent, as if they were not bound to perform any duty unless upon a special motion of the Spirit; but they ought to be diligent in stirring up the grace of God that is in them. . . . We cannot by our best works merit pardon of sin . . . nor satisfy the debt of our former sins, but when we have done all we can, we have done but our duty, and are unprofitable servants: and because, as they [works] are good, they proceed from His Spirit; and as they are wrought by us, they are defiled, and mixed with so much weakness and imperfection [no work is ever perfect in this life; so much for sinlessly abiding in Christ], that they cannot endure the severity of God's judgment (Chapter 16).

CONCERNING PERSEVERANCE: They, whom God hath accepted in His Beloved, effectually called, and sanctified by His Spirit, can neither totally nor finally fall away from the state of grace, but shall certainly persevere therein to the end [not sin all they want], and be eternally saved. This perseverance of the saints *depends not upon their own free will,* but upon the immutability of the decree of election, flowing from the free and unchangeable love of God the Father; upon the efficacy of the merit and intercession of Jesus Christ, the abiding of the Spirit, and of the seed of God within them, and the nature of the covenant of grace: from all which ariseth also the certainty and infallibility thereof. Nevertheless, they may, through the temptations of Satan and of the world, the prevalence of corruption remaining in them, and the neglect of the means of their preservation, fall into grievous sins; and, *for a time* [not indefinitely], continue therein: whereby they incur God's displeasure, and grieve His Holy

Spirit, come to be deprived of some measure of their graces and comforts, have their hearts hardened, and their consciences wounded; hurt and scandalize others, and bring temporal judgments upon themselves (Chapter 17).

It doesn't get any better than that! The balance is that saints sin, but they repent, like King David. God controls the whole process, giving grace to persevere, occasionally withholding it slightly to teach the saint a lesson, but overall effectually enabling the saint to grow in grace. According to Dillow and others, however, the Christian's perseverance is dependent on his will; and since the power for perseverance is dependent on the will of man, he can obviously say No.

Dillow's Position Is Novel
Dillow's position does not represent the historical position of the church, and he even admits such. He claims that both evangelical Arminianism and evangelical Calvinism have missed the truth of Scripture, and that the historic creeds and confessions, drawn up by the best theologians that Christ has given to His church, are in error.

In all candor, it should be observed that this restoration of the so-called lost Gospel is the same claim that the major cults have made, all of whom (Christian Science, Jehovah's Witnesses, Mormons) were founded last century. We must gravely ask: How did the church grow and survive for two thousand years without Dillow's new Gospel? The Reformers preached another Gospel, the Roman Catholic Church preached another Gospel,[8] Arminians preached another Gospel, but now Dillow and Hodges have restored it! Dillow even takes his own DTS professors to task for their distorted Gospel.[9] If the reader thinks I'm being too harsh, this is precisely the charge that Dillow makes against all who either make lordship a part of initial saving faith (p. 10) or a part of continuing faith (p. 12; see also p. 230). All the following, according to him, taught another Gospel: A. W. Pink, John

---

[8]We are not denying that the Roman church preaches another Gospel but that from Dillow's position all these various traditions are heretical.

[9]Thiessen, p. 19, who wrote a theology used at DTS; p. 28, John Witmer, librarian at DTS; p. 195, Stanley D. Toussaint, professor of Bible at DTS.

Calvin, John Owen, Robert L. Dabney, *The Heidelberg Cate-chism*, *The Canons of the Synod of Dort* (1619), *The Gallic Confession* (1559), *The Westminster Confession of Faith*, Baptist theologian A. H. Strong, John H. Gerstner, John Murray, John MacArthur, theologians Charles Hodge, B. B. Warfield, Louis Berkhof, William G. T. Shedd — in short virtually every major evangelical figure in church history is wrong except Dillow. Dillow calls for a "new Reformation" for Western Christianity, with him leading the way, of course (p. 13).

We must drive home the question, What happened to all those Christians who lived for two thousand years before Dillow? Did they go to hell or just forfeit all rewards? As I read the early fathers and Augustine, I see much affinity between them and the Reformed of today, but Dillow cannot make the connection. Historically, Dillow is an aberration, an anti-nomian, and antinomians have always been condemned whenever they have arisen.

As MacArthur has shown in his most excellent sequel to the *Gospel According to Jesus*, *Faith Works*, Dillow's position is unique to dispensationalism on the American continent in the twentieth century. If one looks backward in time or outside dispensational circles or off the American continent, the heresy virtually disappears. Thus we have this arrogant position: only Americans, only dispensationalists, and only a few dispensationalists agree with Dillow.

Unraveling Dillow's Entanglements

One's position is only as good as his logic and the assumptions on which his logic is based. Dillow often commits logical and exegetical errors that he is not aware of, which repeatedly determine his outcome.

Dillow's Logical Fallacies

Attacking the Man
One fallacy is denigrating the men instead of their arguments. Dillow charges his opponents with being dishonest with cer-tain texts to justify a system, but of course he thinks he is

totally honest and objective. He says that "after twenty years of reading the writings of the [Reformed] . . . and interacting personally with their advocates, this writer is convinced that there is something more going on here besides exegesis" (p. 40). The "something more" is allegedly dishonesty.[10] Repeatedly throughout the book he faults the exegesis of others with an evil motive, conditioning the unwary that if they do not accept his bizarre interpretations, they are dishonest. Since no one wants to be dishonest, the naive mistake a moral blast for a solid argument and tend to accept his aberrations.

Consider these slurs against those who disagree with him: "All kinds of twistings and turnings here" (p. 401); "one is reminded of . . . Alice in Wonderland" (p. 259). The attitude Dillow exudes throughout the book is that only he has the truth and any "honest" person should be able to see it. All such statements reveal an arrogant and calloused attitude but do not progress the arguments he is promulgating.

Avoiding the Essence

Because Dillow does not understand the Reformed Faith, he repeatedly misrepresents it. According to Dillow, "entering" the kingdom of God and "inheriting" the kingdom of God are not the same. Supposedly, the former is a gift and the latter is earned by one's works and is a reward. Dillow quotes William G. T. Shedd, a Reformed theologian from last century, as supporting the idea that "inheriting" is a reward and not a gift while "entering" is a gift. When Shedd speaks of "inheriting" as a reward, however, he is light years from Dillow's concept. Shedd says "inheriting" is a reward, but he explains that these works that flow from perseverance are not meritorious. Dillow emphatically claims they are meritorious. Shedd proclaims even of the regenerate: ". . . there is not an absolutely good work to be found in man. . . ."[11] Also according to Shedd, one cannot enter without inheriting since salvation is indivisible. Dillow does not understand Shedd's concept that the works are not meritorious so he has used

---

[10]Dillow's claim to be able to read another's motive may be a violation of the Ninth Commandment, bearing false witness.

[11]William G. T. Shedd, *Dogmatic Theology* (Grand Rapids: Zondervan, 1888, 1969), 2:550; read also pages 549ff.

Shedd's words but not his definitions of his words.

Another example of avoiding the essence is erecting a straw man. Dillow thinks the Reformed men are saying that repentance is a good work, obedience to God, and a pre-condition to prepare oneself for receiving justification. What they actually maintain is that repentance is a mental recognition of our sinfulness and helplessness before God, which has obedience as its fruit. Likewise they say that faith is trust in Jesus which has the same fruit. But Dillow argues for many pages that repentance is mental assent *only*, stating that the Reformed men believe that repentance is works. In fact Dillow's whole book is basically a straw man approach to what the Reformed men are saying.

Accountability Is Not Ability

Another fallacy is basic to Arminians, which is the error that *ought* implies *ability*. If God says one *ought* to do something, that supposedly means he *can* do it. If God commands one to believe in Jesus, he can. Thus since God commands all to believe in Christ, all can; and whoever claims to do so is considered a Christian.[12] If each profession of faith is genuine, what of those who do not persevere? Apparently, they have decided *not* to follow Jesus.[13] Dillow says they have not decided to do so. At every point man is sovereign and God waits to see if man will give Him permission to do something. Man's will is sovereign in his justification and in his sanctification. If man wants justification, he will take it now, but if he does not desire sanctification then God must allow him this privilege. The whole Arminian/humanist scheme is based on an assumption that Scripture specifically denies. God specifically denies that the lost can believe or do anything pleasing to Him.

But the natural man does not receive the things of the Spirit

---

[12]If one were to doubt the professor's faith, that would be tantamount to doubting God's promise that He would save anyone. It is God who is doubted rather than the one who professes faith. The consistent Arminian at least honors God by teaching that the one who does not persevere has lost his salvation while Dillow dishonors God by allowing that he can have his sin and the holy God simultaneously.

[13]This insightful statement comes from my editor, Teresa Johnson.

of God, for they are foolishness to him; *nor can he know them,* because they are spiritually discerned (1 Cor. 2:14).

Because the carnal mind is enmity against God; for it is not subject to the law of God, *nor indeed can be* (Rom. 8:7).

No one *can* come to Me unless the Father who sent Me draws him; and I will raise him up at the last day. It is written in the prophets, "And they shall all be taught by God." Therefore everyone who has heard and learned from the Father comes to Me (John 6:44, 45).

But we are all like an unclean thing, and all our righteousnesses are like filthy rags; we all fade as a leaf, and our iniquities, like the wind, have taken us away. *And there is no one who calls on Your name, who stirs himself up to take hold of You;* for You have hidden Your face from us, and have consumed us because of our iniquities (Isa. 64:6, 7).

Scripture is saying that the lost do not *want* to believe and that they *cannot*. There will never be a person in hell who did not initially want to be there, although God's choice was prior in allowing him to pursue his sinful desires. Likewise, anyone who wants to go to heaven can and will because it was God who gave him the desire and the ability: "Therefore, my beloved, as you have always obeyed, not as in my presence only, but now much more in my absence, work out your own salvation with fear and trembling; *for it is God who works in you both to will and to do* for His good pleasure" (Phil. 2:12, 13). God produces the desire ("to will") and the ability ("to do"). Salvation is *all* of grace.

Man is indeed accountable to God, but this is not the same as ability. In unmistakably clear terms, Paul says: "You will say to me then, 'Why does He *still* find fault? For who has resisted His will?'" (Rom. 9:19). God *still* finds fault, and yet no one is able to resist His will. Responsibility does not imply ability. If Dillow would read the Reformed writers, he would see that these errors were laid to rest centuries ago. Because he does not understand the Reformed position (and the biblical position), he is repeating the errors of the past.

Not only does *ought* entail ability, according to Dillow, but ability limits obligation. Dillow and others say that man must confess all his *known* sins, which implies that he is not accountable for the sins he does not know. His lack of knowledge limits his ability and thus his obligation to God.[14] According to him, sanctification is halted by non-confession of known sin. To enable sanctification to continue if the saint is "out of fellowship" with God, he must confess his *known* sins. If he does not know them, he need not worry about them. Of course, the easy solution to this problem is for the saint to refrain from reading the Bible and going to church so that he will not know what his sins are and thus not be accountable for them.

In Dillow's view since *ought* implies ability, man's will — not God's grace — makes the difference whether one person is converted and another lost. One man "improved"[15] his grace, *allowed* God to save him, and thus "appropriated" God's grace, whereas the others did not. The difference between him and other sinners is found within himself, not in the grace of God. Others had the same opportunity but did not use it wisely as the converted sinner did. They were foolish, but he was wise. They could have merited justification as he did, but they did not. As W. E. Henley stated it, man is "master of his fate" and "captain of his soul."[16] In the anti-lordship position, man determines whether he will be converted and then whether he will be sanctified.

Most Protestants have forgotten that the heart of the Reformation was the battle over "free will," for Luther, Calvin and the others rightly saw that if the efficacy of God's grace were dependent on what man did, even on man's will, then Roman Catholicism was established. All the Reformers emphatically denied that *ought* implied ability. If man could *will* his way into conversion, then why not say — as the Romanists

---

[14]In this thinking, if a man is such a great sinner that he is unable to obey God, then only a mild intent to do right is enough. God's standard is lowered to meet the sinner's lowered ability. We have, therefore, as Warfield noted in *Perfectionism*, the inconceivable conclusion that a sinner who has lived an incredibly wicked life and who is incapable of any good is actually not obligated to do any good. The surest way to heaven, then, would require one to be as wicked as possible so one's liability would be reduced to zero.

[15]A word the Puritans used.

[16]Burton Egbert Stevenson, *The Home Book of Verse* (New York: Holt, Rinehart & Winston, 1965), pp. 3500-3501.

did — that he could *will* all good works and use God's grace to save himself. In short, if God's grace were not irresistible, not a free gift, then God's grace in some form was earned. Luther's *On the Bondage of the Will*, written against Erasmus, and Calvin's *The Eternal Predestination of God*, were both written against the Roman doctrine that man's will is the determining factor in salvation. Virtually all the Reformers wrote against "free will," including John Knox, Bullinger and even the last Puritan, Jonathan Edwards, whose theme verse for his book was Romans 9:16: "So then it is not of him who wills, nor of him who runs, but of God who shows mercy."

Therefore, Dillow is logically inconsistent with what Scripture says about ability and accountability and out of step with the Protestant Reformation. Yet this point, more than anything else, determines what he sees in Scripture.

Amassing Contradictions

Dillow often gives contradictory statements of his position. For example, he argues for 650 pages that works are totally optional for the "believer" but then he states the opposite several times:

> . . . true faith certainly involves a disposition of openness to God and cannot coexist with an attitude of determination to continue in sin (p. 10).

> Those who have been born again will always give some evidence of growth in grace and spiritual interest and commitment. A man who claims to be a Christian and yet never manifests any change at all has no reason to believe he is justified (p. 21).

How can such ideas be harmonized with other statements?

> The automatic unity between justification and sanctification . . . is not taught in Scripture (p. 21).

> A life of good works . . . is not the inevitable outcome (p. 22).

> [One can be carnal and not have any rewards, Chapter 14.]

What is one to make of such statements? Apparently some change is necessary — except when he argues against perseverance. Then no change is necessary. But Dillow states regarding repentance:

It is impossible to become a Christian and at the same time harbor ideas that one is going to "continue in sin." Becoming a Christian involves repentance, a change of perspective about sin, i.e., agreeing with God's perspective about it, that it is sin. . . . Now it is biblically, psychologically, and spiritually impossible to look to the cross for forgiveness and have God's viewpoint about sin and at the same time cherish ideas of intending to persist in some known sin in the life. But that is a completely different thing from saying that, in order to become a Christian, one must commit himself to turning from all known sin, hate his father and mother, and be willing to die for Christ! (p. 151).

His view of repentance is not bad in this quote, though it contradicts his views elsewhere when he emphatically states that the semantic value of the word "repentance" does not allow the theological idea of turning from sin. His paradigm of resistible grace causes such contradictions continually, and he is not aware of it. According to him, one must not embrace sin and Christ and expect to see heaven, but then the rest of the book promotes the idea that one can do just that. Apparently, the Christian cannot view sin as good, but then he can practice it all his life, forfeit all rewards, and still enter heaven. Who can make sense of all works as optional but some change as necessary, of a Christian's obedience as an option but his considering sin from God's view as a necessity, of the impossibility of taking God's view of sin with the intention of continuing in sin but the possibility of not turning from sin?

Asserting Inaccurately

Another logical fallacy is theological imprecision. Often Dillow is ambiguous, which demonstrates that he has not wrestled with some things. For example he says, "It should be pointed out that few follow the Calvinists on this point — that a man can be saved before he believes" (p. 34). What does Dillow mean by "saved," election, justification, sanctification, or glorification? And what does he mean by "*before* he believes," logically or temporally? One is "saved" by election temporally before he believes and logically regenerated before he believes though belief coincides temporally with regeneration, being regeneration's effect. Such ambiguity is a constant problem in his book.

Dillow's Exegetical Fallacies

Optional Covenants

One exegetical assumption pervades Dillow's book: If a New Testament author addresses his audience as "saints," "Christians," or some other such designation, Dillow assumes that it is not possible that they may be unregenerate or at least in doubt. In other words, in Dillow's thinking it is not possible for a Christian author to address other Christians, doubting their salvation. Therefore, we must interpret the rest of the particular book of Scripture as not doubting their salvation; and if it seems as if their salvation is questioned, it must be reinterpreted to mean their rewards are in doubt. This is a presupposition that he does not defend, and it is a false one.

From this it is obvious that he does not understand biblical covenants, which can address those in Scripture as God's people and yet many in the group may not be converted. In 1 Corinthians 10:1ff, Paul states that *all* were baptized into Moses, which initiated them as the people of God, and all ate and drank the same spiritual food, which was Christ. Yet with most of them God was not well pleased because they committed idolatry and many other such sins. Many proved not to be true Israelites, for not all Israel is Israel (Rom. 9:6), and God "having saved the people out of the land of Egypt, afterward destroyed those who did not believe" (Jude 1:4). The whole nation was God's covenant people, yet only some believed. Again, the whole nation belonged to God covenantally (Heb. 3 & 4), yet many hardened their hearts, did not believe the Gospel (Heb. 3:16-4:3), indicated their unbelief by not persevering (Heb. 3:6, 14), and fell away. Could not God address them as His people and yet call for their conversion as He often did in the prophets? The tares grow up with the wheat.

In Galatians Paul wonders if Christ has truly been formed in them or not (Gal. 4:19, 20); in 2 Peter 1 we are told that the saint makes his calling and election sure by perseverance; the Corinthians must examine themselves to see if they are in the faith (2 Cor. 13:5); even Paul must discipline himself lest he become disqualified after he has preached to others

(1 Cor. 9:27); in Hebrews, one can be enlightened, partaker of the Holy Spirit (6:4ff), sanctified by the blood of Jesus (10:29) and not be of those who believe to the saving of the soul (Heb. 10:39).

John tells us in chapter eight that a true Israelite is one who endures (John 8:31; 1 John 2:19). Jesus agreed that the Pharisees were the covenanted seed of Abraham (John 8:37), but a few verses later He also stated that they were not Abraham's children (v. 39) but of their father the devil (v. 44). Indeed, if they were truly Abraham's children, they would do the works of Abraham (v. 39) — and Jesus said all these things to those who had just believed in Him (v. 31). Obviously, Jesus did not accept their profession of faith as genuine. So much for Dillow's assumption that those addressed by the Apostles in their writings cannot be challenged to examine their profession.

Optional Commands

Another assumption Dillow repeatedly invokes is that a command to do something means that those addressed are either not doing it or have the possibility of not doing it all their lives and still be Christians. For example, if Paul commands the Galatians to produce the fruit of the Spirit, then this means that either they were not doing so (why would he command them to do something they were already doing?) or at least had the option not to produce this fruit and still be considered Christians. This assumption leads him to inform Paul's statement that those who practice the works of the flesh will not inherit the kingdom of God to mean that "inheriting" is not the same as "having." Thus by a faulty assumption he interprets whole contexts instead of allowing the contexts to interpret his assumption. The answer is that often commands are given to those who are already doing them to keep them doing them or to tell them that if they do not practice them they reveal an unregenerate heart and will go to hell.

Some sins a Christian cannot even commit, such as the unpardonable sin, and a Christian is not allowed to continue in any sin. One may commit sodomy while a Christian, but if he is unrepentant, unlike King David who committed adultery, he demonstrates an unregenerate heart. Therefore, one must not simply assume that a command is optional or that the readers were not practicing it. The context must determine.[17]

Optional Unity

Though not all dispensationalists follow Dillow's interpretations, Dillow's dispensationalism destroys any semblance of understanding either Scripture or the Reformed Faith. Dispensationalism chops the Bible into a thousand parts, each independent of the others, conveniently making numerous passages irrelevant for today. For example, the strong verses in Matthew 24:13; Revelation 12:17; 13:10 that speak of perseverance are summarily considered irrelevant because these apply to the so-called future tribulation period and not to us today.

Another example is Romans 10:9, 10, which has been rightly used by the church for hundreds of years for justification. Dillow's "ax" (read "disparity hermeneutic") chops the passage to pieces. He does not want it to read that one must

#165; F. Blass and A. Debrunner, *A Greek Grammar of the New Testament and Other Early Christian Literature* (Chicago: The University of Chicago Press, 1970), #335.

[18]Remember, he prides himself in his "literal" method of interpreting, saying that only dispensationalists use the proper hermeneutic.

third concept: "physical deliverance from the future day of wrath upon the earth and the restoration of the Jews to Palestine and not deliverance from hell." Within five verses his lack of unity in interpretation leads him to three different ideas, and to very little having to do with the context. Quoting the verses is sufficient to refute this:

> (9) that if you confess with your mouth Jesus as Lord and believe in your heart that God has raised Him from the dead, you will be saved. (10) For with the heart one believes to righteousness, and with the mouth confession is made to salvation. (11) For the Scripture says, "Whoever believes on Him will not be put to shame." (12) For there is no distinction between Jew and Greek, for the same Lord over all is rich to all who call upon Him. (13) For "whoever calls upon the name of the Lord shall be saved" (Rom. 10:9-13).

The context is salvation or justification (vv. 2-5), and Paul states that the one who confesses Jesus as Lord will be "saved," which he defines as receiving righteousness, further explaining that believing in Him is "calling on His name." Obviously, Dillow is blatantly wrong.

Dillow's slicing the Bible up leads him to charge the Reformed men with using the analogy of faith, which is another way to say the Reformed men assume the unity of the Bible in interpretation. Dillow refers to the analogy of faith method as a "theological hermeneutic." This is a dishonest approach, according to him, in which one interprets passages in light of other passages, or interprets passages from a theology already derived rather than allowing the texts to develop one's theology. But if we believe that Scripture does not contradict itself, this method is unavoidable, especially using clearer passages to interpret the more obscure. Furthermore, one's theology is always being used to interpret Scripture and also using Scripture to change one's theology. The question is not whether to use this method but whether one is consciously aware of this process, always seeking to conform his theology with the Bible. As we shall see in the example on "inheriting the kingdom," Dillow also uses other passages in his interpretations, which we will discuss under the following heading.

Optional Holiness: An Example of Dillow's Faulty Interpretation ("Inheriting the Kingdom")

An example of Dillow's method of interpretation is his understanding of Galatians 5:21 and 1 Corinthians 6:9, 10 that say that those who practice unrighteousness will not inherit the kingdom of God. Hodges's reply is that *inheriting* is not the same as *entering*,[19] but *inheriting* refers to obtaining a reward by works.[20] Dillow holds the same (chs. 3-5). Yet we encounter such passages as "it is through many tribulations that we *enter* the kingdom of God" (Acts 14:22). Paul preached *about* the kingdom of God (Acts 19:8) and *just* the kingdom of God (Acts 20:25; 28:23, 31) with no hint of such a casuistical distinction. Also Paul speaks of "inheriting" the kingdom of God in 1 Corinthians 15:50 as the same as "entering" it, of no immoral person "inheriting" the kingdom in Ephesians 5:5, and then adds in verse 6: "Let no one deceive you with empty words, for because of these things *the wrath of God* comes upon *the sons of disobedience*." Do Hodges and Dillow also maintain that there is a wrath of God on true believers and that they are called "sons of disobedience"? In short we are *transferred* into the kingdom of Christ (Col. 1:13), *called* into this kingdom (1 Thess. 2:12), *considered worthy* of the kingdom (2 Thess. 1:5), *enter* the kingdom (Acts 14:22), and *inherit* the kingdom (1 Cor. 6:9, 10; Gal. 5:21; Eph. 5:5), with little or no distinction between the expressions.

Dillow does not think that we can use so many diverse contexts to interpret "inheritance." He says that each context must stand alone, assuming diversity rather than unity.[21] Quoting approvingly James Barr in *The Semantics of Biblical Language*, he says that we cannot add up meanings from various contexts when we study a word (such as *inheritance*) and then give the meaning of the word as the sum total of all the contexts. This isolation method of interpretation is a major point of his book that he repeatedly invokes in which each context must stand alone. Consequently, his hermeneu-

---

[19]Zane Hodges, *The Hungry Inherit* (Chicago: Moody Press, 1972), p. 115.

[20]Hodges, p. 116.

[21]It is not possible to assume nothing, for one either assumes the unity or diversity of Scripture.

tic leads him to find myriad distinctions where none exist.

I also have read James Barr's book, twice in fact. Barr is a staunch liberal, who thinks that the Bible should be studied by the same method as any other book. His criticisms of doing word studies and especially of the *Theological Dictionary of the New Testament*, however, have some merit. It is true that often people look up a word in its various contexts and sum up all the data and then conclude that the sum total is the meaning in each context. This is not always a correct method, as Barr correctly demonstrates. Barr's liberalism, however, has pushed him to another extreme, to which Dillow and some DTS men have gravitated, which is a denial of the analogy of Scripture. It is thinking that *only* the semantic value of a word is the legitimate meaning, tending to avoid the theological meaning of words.

An example will help to understand Barr's and Dillow's mistake. The semantic value of "God" is a supreme being without saying who He is or anything about Him. If we were to follow Dillow's method, the word "God" in the Bible would only mean this one thing without implying which God or His characteristics. Who would deny, though, that this Greek word, when used in the New Testament, does not mean Zeus or Apollo but the sovereign Triune God who eternally exists in three Persons who are the same in substance, equal in power and glory? Of course, the context will tell us if "God" refers to the Father, the Son, the Holy Spirit, or all Three, but the point is that we must take other usages under consideration to understand the term "God" in the Bible.

It is quite impossible for one who believes in inerrancy to reject the analogy of faith method of interpreting the Bible, for if we believe that Scripture does not contradict itself (and it does not!), then we must use the clearer passages to interpret the parts that are not as clear and use the theological understanding of words — such as "God" — to interpret the Bible properly. If Paul says that we are not justified by works (Eph. 2:8, 9) and promotes a salvation that includes good works (Eph. 2:10), we look for harmony. If Paul says we are justified by faith alone in Christ alone and James says we are justified by works, we seek a solution. (The solution is easy: the kind of faith that justifies is a working faith.) When terms like "God," "promise," and "inheritance" are used, which are often in contexts of justification, we look for theological meanings. To do less is to miss what God is saying.

The reason James Barr refuses so tenaciously to understand words in the Bible in their theological sense by "summing up" their meanings or by analogy is that he does not believe the Bible is God's Word. Since the Bible was written by men who often contradicted both their own writings and the writings of other Apostles, one cannot assume that the usage of "inheritance" would be consistent from writer to writer. Therefore, one can only rely on the semantic value of a word in its immediate context. Paul may contradict Peter, and Paul may contradict himself from one New Testament epistle to another. Consequently, to assume harmony is irrational to him. Barr, as a liberal, has gone to one extreme, and Dillow, who is not liberal, has adopted his method. Yet there are times when Dillow uses other parts of the Bible to understand a passage, and these are usually when his square peg theology will not fit in the round hole of the text.

The other extreme is to deny that there are distinctions in meanings between common words used from biblical author to biblical author, and sometimes even within one author. The balance is not to predefine how to interpret the Bible, as Dillow does, but to allow the Bible to interpret itself, assuming its consistency.

Dillow is harsh on the Reformed men for using the analogy approach, while he invokes the Old Testament theological meaning of "inheritance" to misconstrue the New Testament's view that one who practices the works of the flesh will not inherit the kingdom of God (Gal. 5:21; 1 Cor. 6:9; Eph. 5:5). To Dillow these New Testament passages simply mean that one may not have rewards. He arrives at this because the Old Testament allegedly viewed the saints as having two inheritances: one by faith and one by works. The faith inheritance in the Old Testament was to have God Himself and the works inheritance was to have the land of Palestine. Similarly, according to Dillow, the New Testament saints will have eternal life by faith and the millennial land-rest by their works. Dillow has "added up" the Old Testament meanings of inheritance to force the New Testament concept into his theological mold. Thus when a New Testament passage says one inherits by faith, this is grace inheritance (justification); and when another passage attributes inheritance to perseverance, this is a merited inheritance (millennial rest). He has used an Old Testament theological paradigm to predetermine the meaning of "inheritance" in the New Testament, quite apart from its semantical meaning, but he absolutely denies others the right to use the same approach. If they do, they are dishonest, trying to justify a system.

Read these passages, however, and see if there is a difference between various kinds of inheriting:

> Do you not know that the unrighteous will not *inherit* the kingdom of God? Do not be deceived. Neither fornicators, nor idolaters, nor adulterers, nor homosexuals, nor sodomites, nor thieves, nor covetous, nor drunkards, nor revilers, nor extortioners will *inherit* the kingdom of God. And such were [not now] some of you. But you were washed, but you were sanctified, but you were justified in the name of the Lord Jesus and by the Spirit of our God (1 Cor. 6:9-11).

> For if the *inheritance* (is) of the law, (it is) no longer of promise; but God gave (it) to Abraham by promise. And if you (are) Christ's, then you are Abraham's seed, and heirs according to the promise (Gal. 3:18, 29).

> Now the works of the flesh are evident, which are: adultery, fornication, uncleanness, licentiousness, idolatry, sorcery, hatred, contentions, jealousies, outbursts of wrath, selfish ambitions, dissensions, heresies, envy, murders, drunkenness, revelries, and the like; of which I tell you beforehand, just as I also told (you) in time past, that those who practice such things will not *inherit* the kingdom of God (Gal. 5:19-21).

> In whom also we have obtained an *inheritance*, being predestined according to the purpose of Him who works all things according to the counsel of His will, who is the guarantee of our *inheritance* until the redemption of the purchased possession, to the praise of His glory (Eph. 1:11, 14).

> For this you know, that no fornicator, unclean person, nor covetous man, who is an idolater, has any *inheritance* in the

kingdom of Christ and God (Eph. 5:5).

Giving thanks to the Father who has qualified us to be partakers of the *inheritance* of the saints in the light (Col. 1:12).

That having been justified by His grace we should become *heirs* according to the hope of eternal life (Titus 3:7).

Blessed (be) the God and Father of our Lord Jesus Christ, who according to His abundant mercy has begotten us again to a living hope through the resurrection of Jesus Christ from the dead, to an *inheritance* incorruptible and undefiled and that does not fade away, reserved in heaven for you (1 Peter 1:3, 4).

Are they not all ministering spirits sent forth to minister for those who will *inherit* salvation? (Heb. 1:14).

That you do not become sluggish, but imitate those who through faith and patience *inherit* the promises (Heb. 6:12).

And for this reason He is the Mediator of the new covenant, by means of death, for the redemption of the transgressions under the first covenant, that those who are called may receive the promise of the eternal *inheritance* (Heb. 9:15).

By faith Noah, being divinely warned of things not yet seen, moved with godly fear, prepared an ark for the saving of his household, by which he condemned the world and became *heir* of the righteousness which is according to faith. By faith Abraham obeyed when he was called to go out to the place which he would (afterward) receive as an *inheritance*. And he went out, not knowing where he was going. By faith he sojourned in the land of promise as (in) a foreign country, dwelling in tents with Isaac and Jacob, the *heirs* with him of the same promise; for he waited for the city which has foundations, whose builder and maker (is) God (Heb. 11:7-10).

We become heirs by predestination, by faith, by promise, and by perseverance, and in each context the grace of God produces the results. To think, as Dillow does, that we interpret words and ideas in isolation is to promote a Bible that has scattered truths that are unrelated like beads spilled on a floor. Rather the Bible is like beads that are strung together, like white light that a prism can break into its various hues, each "bead" or "beam" being part of the whole. Like the prism, we can analyze the Bible's teachings and categorize them, but we are never to think of them as independent of one another. Indeed, the "beads" are strung into a unity because God is one. Each part of the Bible implies the rest, and no truth is to be isolated from any other truth. If one inheritance is by faith and the other is by works and if the works are optional, we have two "beads" that are unrelated.

But that "inheritance" in the New Testament can mean the same as justification is seen further (besides the many passages just quoted) in the lexicons, which define "inheritance" as justification, listing these passage as examples: Acts 20:32; Gal. 3:18; Col. 3:24; Eph. 1:14, 18; 5:5; Heb. 9:15; 1 Peter 1:4 (Arndt and Gingrich lexicon).

Do Paul or the other Apostles give any clue that they adhere to two kinds of inheritance? Not at all. Why do these verses lead Dillow to see two different kinds of inheritance? Why not five kinds? His paradigm calls for two: one by faith and one by works. It is obvious that this assumed dichotomy between faith and works is giving him this myopia so that he only sees according to the "glasses" (read assumptions) he is wearing. It is not wrong, of course, to wear "glasses;" in fact, it is impossible not to wear them, but one must be consciously aware of them and constantly test them by Scripture. Even the claim to be completely neutral is an assumption.

Christ is a unit, salvation is a unit, faith/repentance is a unit so that God can view a sinner's salvation from eternity (Eph. 1:4, 5), from Christ's death (Eph. 1:7, 8), from the immediate application to the believer (Eph. 1:13, 14), from justification (Rom. 5:1), or from the fruit from sanctification (Rom. 6-8). At any point God, through one of His human authors of Scripture, can say one is not a Christian, for one either has all of salvation or none of it. If one is not elect, he is not a Christian (Rom. 11:7-10; Matt. 11:25-27); if he is not justified he is not a Christian (John 3:36); or if he is not being sanctified he is not a Christian (Rom. 6:15-21; 7:1-13; 8:4-17; 1 John 2:3, 4; 3:9-15). Likewise, inheritance may be viewed from election, from faith, from promise, of from perseverance, but it is a unit. *It is only when salvation is segmented into optional parts that lordship salvation is a problem and that Scrip-*

ture seems difficult to harmonize.

Dillow is just plain wrong about the meaning of "inheritance." In Matthew 19 and Mark 10, the rich young ruler considered entering heaven, inheriting eternal life, and having eternal life all the same; and Jesus did not correct him. Indeed, the rich young ruler was confronted with the lordship of Jesus, which he refused to accept by refusing to sell all his possessions, indicating that he did not see himself as a sinner (no repentance), and so went away without eternal life.

In another passage (Matt. 25:34), which describes the Last Day judgment, we read:

> Then the King will say to those on His right hand, "Come, you blessed of My Father, *inherit* the kingdom prepared for you from the foundation of the world: for I was hungry and you gave Me food; I was thirsty and you gave Me drink; I was a stranger and you took Me in; I (was) naked and you clothed Me; I was sick and you visited Me; I was in prison and you came to Me."

We have true faith evidenced by what they did, and these people "inherit" the kingdom. That this is not simply rewards is crystal clear a few verses later: "And these will go away into everlasting punishment, but the righteous into eternal life" (Matt. 25:46). Dillow twists the text to try to make this a judgment of rewards and not of eternal salvation, but again there is no need to do this if one understands faith biblically.

In Galatians 3 and 4 one inherits and is an heir by faith in Jesus, which gives him standing as a son. The "inheritance" is not by the law but by promise (3:18), and all men are under sin that the promise might be by faith in Jesus (3:22). We are "sons of God through faith in Christ Jesus" (3:26), which makes us "heirs according to promise" (3:29). And to leave no doubt that all God's sons are heirs, Paul says, "You are no longer a slave, but a son, and if a son, then an heir through Christ" (4:7). And what they inherit is eternal life itself. Here the inheritance is by faith in Jesus, and in Matthew 25 it is by a faith that works. In both cases one receives eternal life.

Repeatedly Dillow interprets passages like these from the assumption that faith does not have works, which is precisely what he is trying to prove. In other words, he is using the analogy of faith to interpret Scripture, allowing one passage to interpret another, which is a good Reformed hermeneutic though he abuses it and condemns the Reformed men for doing the same.

Conclusion

We shall see these theological, logical, and exegetical weaknesses throughout Dillow's work, determining his view, and we shall consider the lordship issue under four heads: regeneration, repentance and faith, justification and sanctification, and assurance of salvation.

2

Regeneration

Dillow does not discuss how regeneration is done or its nature. If the new birth is a sovereign work of God, man does not have a "free will" and grace is irresistible and free. Furthermore, if being born again is not simply the potential for good but actually changes the disposition of the person, perseverance would be the inevitable outcome. In this chapter we shall examine these things.

How Regeneration is Accomplished

Sovereign Regeneration

How is regeneration or the new birth accomplished? Or, How is one born again? Where in the Bible does God tell us how we can be born again? If it is a sovereign work of God, then man is not the determiner of his birth, does not set the date of his regeneration, and therefore is not in control of God. Conversely, if man sets the date of his conversion, then any time he professes faith we must say it is genuine because God is always willing. And what are we to say if he produces no fruit in his life? Dillow and others say that man is equally sovereign over sanctification as in regeneration. The sinner allegedly may take regeneration but reject sanctification.

Is one born again by faith, by God, or by works? No evangelical would say by works, and all evangelicals would say by God. Where does the Bible say we are born again by faith in Christ? This is a false assumption taken for granted. Usually people point to John 3:1-8. But where in the passage did the

Lord tell Nicodemus *how* to be born again? Some say that it is necessary or one could not enter the kingdom, which is true. The word for "must" in John 3 (*dei*) means "it is necessary," but it is not a command to do so. Even if it were, a command does not mean one would have the ability to obey. How could a command to have the new life of regeneration make a dead sinner able to respond? We must observe in John 3 that the Lord thought the Old Testament saints were born again just as New Testament ones, for He said to Nicodemus: "Are you the teacher of Israel, and do not know these things?" (v. 10). He was surprised that Nicodemus would not understand something so basic as the new birth, and this was supposedly still under the dispensation of law, as our dispensational friends would say. Saints from all ages have always been regenerated by the Holy Spirit and permanently indwelt by Him,[1] or else we would have pure Pelagianism: man living a godly life by raw will power and not by the power of the Holy Spirit.

There are no instructions given. Jesus never told Nicodemus how. In fact Nicodemus asked how, even wondering if it would entail re-entering his mother's womb. But the Lord gave His answer in verse 8 when He compared the working of the Spirit to the working of the wind. Just as the wind blows when and where it wills, so the Spirit "blows" or regenerates whom He wills, and just as we see the effect of the wind, so we see the effect of the new birth by the results in the lives of new Christians.

The verb "born" in John 3 is in the passive voice, indicating that it is done by someone other than and outside of the sinner. The word "again" in "born again" usually means "from above," disclosing that it is not a work of man but a sovereign work of God.

Some use John 1:12, saying we become God's children by faith. They say that if we become God's children by faith, we must be born again by faith. However, the next verse clarifies verse 12: "Who were born, not of blood, nor of the will of the flesh, *nor of the will of man*, but of God." The reason the faith in verse 12 exists is that they had been born of God. The Bible does not give instructions regarding the mechanics of the new

---

[1]See appendix 3.

birth.[2]

The syntactical relationship of Greek tenses in 1 John is very instructive.[3] In each of the following passages there is a cause-effect relationship between the perfect and present tenses in Greek. In 2:29 the effect (present tense) of the new birth (perfect tense) is "practicing righteousness." No one but the worst of heretics would say we are born again by our works. In 3:9 the effect (present tense) of the new birth (perfect tense) is "not practicing sin." Again, are we born again by not practicing sin? No. In 4:7 the effect (present tense) of the new birth (perfect tense) is love for the brethren. In 5:4 the effect (present tense) of regeneration (perfect tense) is overcoming the world. Here is the main point: in 5:1 the effect (present tense) of the new birth (perfect tense) is *faith in Christ*. We are not born again by faith in Christ but we have faith because we are born again. The syntax is identical.

James 1:18 is similar: "In the exercise *of His will* He brought us forth [caused us to be born again] by the word of truth." But what is "the word of truth?" The verse emphasizes that it was *He* who brought us forth, by an act of *His* will (see Rom. 9:16) so that the "word of truth" is His sovereign power, such as Jesus calling Lazarus to life by His word. Similarly, 1 Peter 1:3 in the New American Standard Bible brings out the causative force of the verb: "Blessed be the God and Father of our Lord Jesus Christ, who according to His great mercy *has caused* us to be born again."

Another objection is from 1 Peter 1:23: "For you have been born again not of seed which is perishable but imperishable, through the word of God which lives and abides forever."[4] Some conclude that we are born again by believing the word of God or the Gospel. However, Peter is very careful in his use of prepositions: Verse 23 says we are born *from* the

---

[2]The "translation" of the NIV here in rendering "the will of man" as the "will of the husband" is inexcusable. But then this is typical of the NIV.

[3]John Murray in *Redemption Accomplished and Applied* (Wm. B. Eerdmans Pub. Co., 1973), p. 100ff.

[4]The "word" in this verse is the Gospel in verse 25. And even though there are two words for "word" used in these verses, Peter is only quoting the Septuagint and interpreting "word" (*logos*) in verse 23 as the "word" (*rhema*) which is the Gospel in verse 25.

source (*ek*) of the seed and *through* (*dia*) the means of the word. In other words, the seed gives us life which is manifested through our belief in the Gospel, the exact thing John had maintained in 1 John 3:9. The seed is the Holy Spirit (1 John 3:9) and the word is the Gospel. To say we are given life through faith denies the passage; rather, life is manifested through faith. In other words, we are given life immediately by the Holy Spirit, which life is necessarily manifested by believing the Gospel. And just in case we should become hyper-Calvinists, maintaining that some are born again who have not yet believed, 1 John makes it clear that there is no temporal gap between regeneration and belief, for it can be said of every one who has been regenerated that he does not practice sin as a habit, he does practice righteousness, he overcomes the world, and he believes that Jesus is the Christ.

When presented with the truth of God's sovereign, irresistible grace, people often become irrational and retreat to some compromise between God's sovereignty and man's supposed "free will." Very often this solution is what they call an "antinomy," an apparent contradiction to man but not to God. There is no question there are many things about God we do not know (Deut. 29:29), but regeneration is not in that class. People use the antinomy excuse so they can maintain their antinomian license, legalistic merit, or human sovereignty.[5] We have to face facts: God regenerates whom He wills, when He wills.

Of course we preach the Gospel, because 1 Peter 1:23-25 and 1 John indicate that the person believes the Gospel at the point of regeneration, leading us to conclude that regeneration takes place in the context of the preaching of the Gospel. But it is still sovereign. John the Baptist was even regenerated while in his mother's womb.

Some biblical examples will further illustrate these things. In Acts 16:14 "the Lord *opened* her [Lydia] heart to respond to the things spoken by Paul." Did you catch the logical — not temporal — order? The Lord opened her heart (regenerated her) and then she responded (faith) to the things Paul

---

[5]Those who want to dilute the sovereignty passages with so-called "free will" passages do not bring in the sovereignty passages when they encounter an apparent "free will" one.

was preaching. The same can be seen in Acts 13:48: "as many as were ordained to eternal life believed." The ordination gave rise to belief. Likewise Peter says the source of the new birth is the seed or Holy Spirit and the means of manifesting this life is belief in the Gospel (1 Peter 1:23).

Or take the clear example of Lazarus. The miracles in the Gospel of John were done to point to some saving grace in the Lord Jesus (bread of life in feeding five thousand, light of the world in healing the blind man, etc). The Lord had stated that He was calling sinners to life in John 5:25, and in John 11 Jesus claims to be the resurrection and the life. Martha thought He was speaking of the Last Day resurrection, but Jesus meant this for *now* as well as the Last Day. As is so often the case in Scripture, the physical implies the spiritual meaning. To demonstrate His sovereign grace in calling men to spiritual life, He physically raised Lazarus from the dead. Did Lazarus call out to Jesus to raise him? Did Lazarus set the date of his spiritual resurrection? Did Lazarus even have the ability to blink his eyes? To all the questions, the answer is a resounding No! Lazarus was dead in his sins (Eph. 2:1). Did this hinder Jesus? Not in the least. By name and with creative power, He called Lazarus to physical life, forever illustrating His ability to call dead sinners (Eph. 2:1ff) to spiritual life. Do you think Lazarus ever considered going back to the grave? No, and neither does the regenerate sinner.

One of the best illustrations comes from James Montgomery Boice. He said that preaching the Gospel is like tossing torches in 55 gallon drums. You toss a torch in one drum and there is water in the drum so the torch goes out. The same happens with another drum. Then a torch is cast into a drum with gun powder in it — boom! An explosion occurs. So it is with preaching. We preach and preach and nothing happens; the word falls on deaf ears that cannot — and will not — hear. Then God regenerates one and boom, conversion occurs.

There are times when Dillow seems to opt for the Arminian position that we are born again by faith and times when he leans toward the Reformed position that faith arises from regeneration. Notice these contradictory quotes:

The mere presence of faith in the life is the *evidence* of

regeneration [emphasis added] (p. 290).

> Entrance is ours through rebirth (John 3:5) which is ours solely through believing on His name (John 1:12-13) (p. 78).

His constant assumption, however, is that man is in control and that the sinner is born again by faith.

Objections to Sovereign Regeneration

There are several common objections to God's sovereign grace, and they are answered in Romans 9. First, they say that God only *foreknew* who would accept Him and thus chose those who had first chosen Him (see John 15:16: "You did *not* choose Me"), but Paul says of Esau and Jacob: "For the children not yet being born, nor having done any good or evil, that the purpose of God according to election might stand, not of works but of Him who calls, it was said to her, 'The older shall serve the younger'" (vv. 11, 12). Notice that neither one had done anything, which included choosing Him; it was God's purpose according to election that made the discriminating difference.

Secondly, we hear people say "That's not fair! This would make God unjust." Paul knows that his teaching leads to this objection so he responds:

> What shall we say then? Is there unrighteousness with God? Certainly not! For He says to Moses, 'I will have mercy on whomever I will have mercy, and I will have compassion on whomever I will have compassion.' So then it is *not of him who wills*, nor of him who runs, but of God who shows mercy and on whom He does not. Therefore *He has mercy on whom He wills, and whom He wills He hardens* (vv. 14-16, 18).

Why is this not unfair? Because God said it was not. Paul does not really answer the question but proclaims that the choice is His. With this we must be satisfied (Deut. 29:29).

Thirdly, they object, "If this is so, then God cannot find fault with anyone because they are only doing His will. If they sin, it is His fault for making them do it." Paul responds,

> You will say to me then, "Why does He *still* find fault? For who has resisted His will?" But indeed, O man, who are you to reply against God? Will the thing formed say to him who

formed it, 'Why have you made me like this?' Does not the potter have power over the clay, from the same lump to make one vessel for honor and another for dishonor? (vv. 19-21).

Again Paul knows that what he is teaching leads to this objection, but he says that *we do not have the right to judge God!*

Another objection is: "What about all the *whosoever will* passages?" The answer is simple. All these passages tell us who *will* be saved *if* they believe, not who *can* believe. If we promised a million dollars to anyone who would keep the Ten Commandments perfectly for one year, does the offer confer on the listener the ability to keep the commandments? No. It is a promise to anyone *if* he can do it. Strictly speaking, God does not "offer" salvation in the sense of pleading with sinners, but He *commands* sinners to repent (Acts 17:30; 20:21).[6]

The Bible says against "free will." Scripture is so replete with examples that sometimes when I speak on this I ask the audience from the pulpit for their favorite New Testament books, and then I read passage after passage from their chosen books to show that God irresistibly enables us to believe the Gospel. Here are a few:

> But you do not believe, *because you are not of My sheep,* as I said to you. My sheep hear My voice, and I know them, and they follow Me (John 10:26, 27).

> Therefore *they could not believe*, because Isaiah said again: "He has blinded their eyes and hardened their heart, lest they should see with their eyes and understand with their heart, lest they should turn, so that I should heal them" (John 12:39, 40).

> At that time Jesus answered and said, "I thank You, Father, Lord of heaven and earth, because *You have hidden these things from the wise and prudent and have revealed them to babes.* Even so, Father, for so it seemed good in Your sight. All things have been delivered to Me by My Father, and no one knows the Son except the Father. *Nor does anyone know the Father except the Son, and he to whom the Son wills to reveal Him*" (Matt. 11:25-27).

---

[6]"Whosoever will" may come because whosoever may will come.

And when he desired to cross to Achaia, the brethren wrote, exhorting the disciples to receive him; and when he arrived, he greatly helped those *who had believed through grace* (Acts 18:27).

He chose us in Him *before the foundation of the world*, that we should be holy and without blame before Him in love (Eph. 1:4).

For to you *it has been granted* on behalf of Christ, not only *to believe in Him*, but also to suffer for His sake (Phil. 1:29).

Who has saved us and called us with a holy calling, not according to our works, but according to His own purpose and grace *which was given to us in Christ Jesus before time began* (2 Tim. 1:9).

They stumble, being disobedient to the word, *to which they also were appointed* (1 Peter 2:8).

What Regeneration Does

If regeneration is only the adding of an additional nature, as Dillow assumes, the Christian has two natures. This is turn leads to the idea that the Christian can choose between either nature, functioning this moment by the new nature and that moment by the old nature. Once again the choice is the Christian's. There is a neutral "I" vacillating between two extremes. Such is Dillow's view.

By contrast the Bible teaches that in regeneration the person is passive while God does an immediate work on the soul. Part of the effect of this work is belief in Jesus. In believing, the person is active. In addition the person himself is completely changed. God cleans up, the source of an evil life, the heart,[7] which in turn causes the mind to think righteous thoughts and the will to chose righteously. Not only is regeneration sovereign, but it also a comprehensive work, extending to every part of the soul. Our anti-lordship friends could be cured of a great deal of their problem if only they understood the nature of the new birth. Repeatedly I heard

---

[7]Often in Scripture the heart is the mind, but sometimes also it is the basic nature of the person (Jer. 17:9; 31:33; Ez. 36:25-26; Mark 7:21).

in seminary that the new birth is only the insertion of something new and not the changing of the real "I." To restate this
in their terms, regeneration adds to the person another
nature, leaving the sinful nature intact, with the alleged result
that the new nature cannot be lessened and the old nature
cannot be improved.[8]

Now this is a half truth, often the most dangerous type of
error. It is true that something new is introduced, life from
God, so that the person is alive toward God for the first time.
In addition, though, the soul is transformed. Louis Berkhof's
Systematic Theology has the best definition of regeneration we
have read: "In this sense of the word regeneration may be
defined as that act of God by which the principle of new life
is implanted in man, and the governing disposition of the soul
is made holy. In principle it affects the whole man: the
intellect (1 Cor. 2:14, 15; 2 Cor. 4:6; Eph. 1:18; Col. 3:10), the
will (Phil. 2:13; 2 Thess. 3:5; Heb. 13:21), and the emotions
(Ps. 42:1, 2; Matt. 5:4; 1 Peter 1:8)" (p. 468ff). In short,
regeneration is the change, the permanent renovation, of the
moral disposition of the soul from an orientation to sin to an
orientation to holiness in addition to the introduction of
spiritual life.

We shall consider a few passages confirming the nature
of regeneration. In Hebrews 8:10, which quotes Jeremiah
31:33, God states that He shall write His laws on the hearts
of His people, which is a clear statement that they shall do the
laws. In Ezekiel 36:26-27 it is further stated that the regenerate
have the old heart taken away. Second Corinthians 5:17 says
that all things have become new and that the old things have
passed away.[9]

It is not true that the regenerate person has two natures,
a new nature and an old one. In regeneration the *person himself*
is changed, not simply something added to the person leaving

---

[8]We cannot go into all the ramifications of such a monstrosity in this review so
the reader is encouraged to read Warfield's classic work: *Perfectionism*. R. L.
Dabney observed the same confusion in his day among the Plymouth Brethren,
the precursors to the modern day dispensationalists: *Discussions*, vol. 1, p. 190ff.
Regeneration is, of course, also instantaneous and irreversible.

[9]The critical text says "new things have come," but the majority text more
accurately represents the original which says "all things have become new."

him unchanged. It is the *regenerate* who are being changed into the image of Christ (2 Cor. 4:15-18), not some abstract new nature.

To say the regenerate only have one nature is not to say that we do not have indwelling sin. We struggle every day of our lives with indwelling sin, even as Paul did in Romans 7:14ff. The one who ceases struggling indicates that he loves his sin, that he does not love God, that he has not truly been born again (1 John 2:29). In regeneration God reaches behind the intellect, will, and affections and cleans up the source so that now the saint does what John says in 1 John (practicing righteousness, overcoming the world, believing that Jesus is the Christ).

> Now by this we know that we know Him, if we keep His commandments. He who says, "I know Him," and does not keep His commandments, is a liar, and the truth is not in him (1 John 2:3-4).

> If you know that He is righteous, you know that everyone who practices righteousness is born of Him (1 John 2:29).

> Whoever has been born of God does not sin, for His seed remains in him; and he cannot sin, because he has been born of God (1 John 3:9).

> Beloved, let us love one another, for love is of God; and everyone who loves is born of God and knows God. He who does not love does not know God, for God is love (1 John 4:7-8).

The problem with the sinner before regeneration was a wicked soul, a bad heart. He did not want God (will), did not think of God (mind), and hated Him and His people (affections). All these things — and more — came from within, out of the heart (Mark 7:21ff). Man could not morally change himself anymore than a leopard could change his spots (Jer. 13:23) or man cannot even reach out to Jesus. Everything that came out of him without exception was sin: "Then the Lord saw that the wickedness of man was great in the earth, and that *every* intent of the thoughts of his heart was *only* evil *continually*" (Gen. 6:5). From this verse the natural man is sinful without exception ("every" intent), without mixture ("only" evil), and without intermission ("continually"). So in the new birth God cleans up the mouth of the stream (heart or basic nature) so that it will be clean downstream (mind, will, affections). Therefore, there cannot be any such thing as a regenerate person who does not choose righteously as the characteristic of his life (1 John 3:9), for his mind, will, and affections have a renewed source from which to draw. Regeneration cleans up the person, and this instantaneous and irreversible act is continued in progressive sanctification the rest of his life and concluded in glorification. Indeed, a Christian can sin to his heart's content, for now his heart does not willingly embrace sin.

And why did God use the illustration of new birth except to show that *He* does it and that the person born is *new*? Just as we did not choose to be born, so He chose to give us new life; and just as our first birth produced a new person, so does the second birth.

God does not violate the will of man in regeneration, for prior to being born again, he chooses that which he wants: Satan and sin. His heart is only evil so this is his only choice. In regeneration God moves behind the will to clean up that which determines how the will chooses so that afterwards he chooses that which he wants: Jesus and holiness (1 John 2:29; 3:9; 4:7-8; 5:1). Yet because regenerate man still has the remnants of sin within, he struggles with indwelling sin all his life (Rom. 7:14ff). His overruling disposition, however, is toward holiness.

Take special note of 1 John 3:9, where John says those born of God *cannot* live a life of sin anymore: "Whoever has been born of God does not [practice] sin, for His seed remains in him; and he cannot [practice] sin, because he has been born of God." John is not presenting sinless perfectionism because in 2:1-2 he says Jesus is the propitiation for sinning Christians. John Calvin's commentary on 3:9 cannot be improved.

> . . . [some] imagine such a motion of the Spirit as leaves to us the free choice of good and evil. Hence they draw forth merits, because we willingly obey the influence of the Spirit, which it is in our power to resist. In short, they desire the grace of the Spirit to be only this, that we are enabled to choose right if we will. John speaks far otherwise; for he not only shows

that we cannot sin, but also that the power of the Spirit is so effectual, that it necessarily retains us in continual obedience to righteousness. Nor is this the only passage of Scripture which teaches us that the will is so formed that it cannot be otherwise than right. For God testifies that he gives a new heart to his children . . . that they may walk in His commandments. John not only shows how efficaciously God works once in man, but plainly declares that the Spirit continues His grace in us to the last, so that inflexible perseverance is added to newness of life. Let us not imagine . . . that it is some neutral movement, which leaves men free either to follow or to reject; but let us know that our own hearts are so ruled by God's Spirit that they cleave to righteousness.[10]

God has reached behind the will and changed the basic evil nature, that which governs the motives of the will and its choices. Furthermore, the Holy Spirit rules the Christian. Dillow wants 1 John 3:9 to refer only to the so-called "new" nature, but John is clear when he uses the masculine pronoun to refer to the person: "The *one who* has been born again cannot practice sin." Furthermore, John contrasts the devil's people with God's people — not the so-called dual natures of Christians (1 John 3:4-10).[11]

In conclusion the license view (or Keswick view) says that the person has something new added to him, a new nature. The "I" remains unchanged. The believer has the Spirit "provided," and He may or may not give grace to the Christian, depending on whether the believer fulfills some command. The "I" may function by either nature at any given moment. If the "I" decides to "yield" to the Spirit,[12] then the Spirit flows "through" him, living the life of Christ through the Christian. In other words, one must do good to become good, rather than the biblical teaching that one must first be good to do good works. The view that our choices make us

---

[10]*Calvin's Commentaries*, translated by the Rev. John Owen, volume XXII (Grand Rapids: Baker Book House, 1979), p. 213-14.

[11]Regeneration has many figures in the Bible: new heart, born again, made alive, law written on the heart, etc.

[12]When I was in dispensationalism, I never could get a definition of what it meant to "yield." I went to a pastor in Memphis once, and he said I would just know when I matured enough!

what we are rather than reflect what we are is Pelagianism.

Substitutionary sanctification is not biblical, for the "I" is never changed, but must get out of the way so the Spirit can work "through" the new nature, and as water flows through a tube leaving it unchanged, so allegedly the Spirit flows through the new nature, leaving the believer unchanged. Exactly what is being conformed to the image of Christ is never clear, for the "I" remains unchanged. Remember, according to this view, the new nature cannot be lessened and the old nature cannot be improved. As Warfield so accurately stated of this,[13] when the person is perfected at glorification, the old self is not the one saved, cleaned up, and purified but a new self added that never needed saving at all. But according to Dillow and Keswick theology, if the person functions through the new nature, the works are perfect; if through the old nature, the works are wholly evil. By contrast Reformed theologian John Gerstner says: "For the Reformed theologian, good works, while the *result* of divine grace, are genuinely human actions. For the antinomian, good works *are* divine actions, the direct action of God within the human person" [emphasis his].[14]

With Dillow and others, we have a gnostic dualism with the heavenly not able to affect the earthly. There are allegedly two kinds of faith, a faith without works and a faith with works. This leads to a new birth that only inserts something new, which in turn gives rise to two kinds of Christians: the spiritual and the carnal. Then there are two spheres in salvation: the position and the practice. In "salvation" we can have justification without sanctification. In heaven there are two kinds of Christians: those with rewards and those without them. In each case we have two spheres, functioning like parallel railroad tracks, neither sphere influencing the other.[15]

In the Reformed view, the heavenly is effectual regarding

---

[13]See appendix 2.

[14]John H. Gerstner, *Wrongly Dividing the Word of Truth* (Brentwood, TN: Wolgemuth & Hyatt, 1991), p. 212. See also R. L. Dabney in *Discussions*, vol. 1, p. 190ff.

[15]The reader must read this book to see how gnostic Dillow and his followers are: Philip J. Lee, *Against the Protestant Gnostics* (New York: Oxford University Press, 1987).

the earthly: the Christian not only has life given to him, but the disposition of the soul has a new orientation — obedience to God. The "I" is indeed changed but he has only one nature — humanity. *He* has been regenerated, and this regeneration is continued in progressive sanctification. And *he* is being conformed to Christ; the old man or indwelling sin is being progressively removed. Since the "I" is being changed, there is no substitutionary sanctification. The "I" does not remove itself, for *he* is being sanctified, and the "I" is producing the good works that are the fruit of grace, which good works are not perfect but are accepted for Christ's sake. His faith joins him to Christ, from Whom he receives both justification and sanctification. In union with Christ, how could he possibly receive one without the other? There is no formula to obey to receive power, for the Holy Spirit is always sanctifying the believer and the saint cannot stop His work in himself. Justification necessarily brings about sanctification as the heavenly necessarily affects the earthly.

Conclusion

Regeneration, then, has two aspects: It is done by God on whom He wills, and it changes the person so thoroughly that he is both willing and able (by the Holy Spirit of course) to believe in Jesus and practice the commands of God, though he cannot do so perfectly until he is glorified at death (1 John 3:2). And if regeneration is not allowed by man but sovereignly done by God the Holy Spirit, and if it produces both faith and works, is it not patently obvious that these are the gift of God to His elect, and thus not merited? Perseverance in faith and holiness, therefore, is inevitable.

3

Repentance & Faith

Evangelicals have taught for centuries that faith and repentance are two sides of one coin, that faith involves not only the mind but also the will in embracing Christ, and that repentance means a recognition of one's sins and turning from them. Such concepts of faith and repentance would necessitate perseverance if the person had truly repented and believed in Jesus. Of course if Dillow is to deny perseverance, he must deny the evangelical understanding of repentance and faith.

What is Repentance?

The issue is over the meaning of repentance and faith and whether repentance is necessary for justification. Dillow teaches that repentance is not necessary for justification. His argument is that repentance is a change of mind but does not involve any fruit in one's life, which is a half-truth. It is a change of mind, and if the mind is truly changed, it will have fruit.

We can pursue both the nature and necessity of repentance together. There are two avenues in defining repentance: lexicons and biblical usage. First the lexicons: Arndt and Gingrich Greek lexicon (first edition) defines repentance as "the beginning of a new religious and moral life" (p. 513). Thayer's lexicon is even more detailed: ". . . especially the change of mind of those who have begun to abhor their errors and misdeeds, and have determined to enter upon a better course of life, so that it embraces both a recognition of sin and sorrow for it and hearty amendment, the *tokens and effects* of which are good deeds" [emphasis added] (p. 406).

The Greek words for repentance are used in the Septua-gint (Greek translation of the Old Testament done about 200 B.C.) almost exclusively of the Hebrew word *nacham*, which the Brown, Driver, Briggs Hebrew lexicon defines as "to be sorry for" and thus to turn from sin. Another Hebrew word for repent is *shub*, which the same lexicon explains as "to turn from" sin. Thus the Hebrew and Greek lexicons present repentance as a turning from sin with a corresponding change in one's life. Thus repentance definitely eliminates "easy believism."

The second avenue in defining repentance is the biblical usage, which is found in both Testaments.

> But if the wicked man *turns from all his* sins which he has committed and observes all My statutes and practices justice and righteousness, he shall surely live; he shall not die. Repent and turn from all your transgressions, so that iniquity may not become a stumbling block to you (Ez. 18:21, 30).

> Repent therefore and return, that your sins may be wiped away. He sent Him [Jesus] to bless you *by turning every one from your wicked ways* (Acts 3:19, 26).

> I am sending you to open their eyes so that they *may turn from darkness to light* and from the dominion of Satan to God, in order that they may receive forgiveness of sins and an inheri-tance among those who have been sanctified by faith in Me. I kept declaring . . . that they should *repent and turn to God, performing deeds appropriate to repentance* (Acts 26:17, 18, 20). [The deeds demonstrate that one has repented; they are not the cause but the effect, not the root but the fruit.]

> The time is fulfilled, and the kingdom of God is at hand; *repent and believe* the gospel (Mark 1:15). [Note here that repentance and faith occur together].

> I tell you, no, but, unless you *repent*, you will all likewise perish (Luke 13:3).

> And He said to them, "Thus it is written, that the Christ should suffer and rise again from the dead the third day; and *that repentance and forgiveness of sins* on the basis of His name to all nations — beginning from Jerusalem" (Luke 24:46, 47). [Observe that repentance is to be proclaimed to all nations,

which would include the Gentiles, and it is for forgiveness of sins!]

Therefore *bring forth fruit in keeping with repentance* (Matt. 3:8).

Then Peter said to them, "Repent, and let every one of you be baptized in the name of Jesus Christ for the remission of sins; and you shall receive the gift of the Holy Spirit" (Acts 2:38).

If therefore God gave them the same gift as He gave us when we believed on the Lord Jesus Christ, who was I that I could withstand God? When they heard these things they became silent; and they glorified God, saying, "Then God has also granted to the Gentiles *repentance to life*" (Acts 11:17-18).[1]

Testifying to Jews, and also to Greeks, *repentance toward God and faith* toward our Lord Jesus Christ (Acts 20:21).

From these verses repentance is a "turning from sin" and a condition for forgiveness of sins.

Dillow strongly objects, maintaining that the biblical words for repentance mean a change of mind without turning from one's sins. The lexicons and biblical usage reveal that Dillow makes a false distinction by thinking the change of mind has nothing to do with resultant obedience. Repentance is indeed primarily a change of mind, but one cannot have this change of mind and still love his sins. As we can see from the verses above, it is a change of mind regarding oneself, one's sin, God, and Christ; and if one does not manifest the corresponding behavior, obviously his mind was not changed. Did Luke not say in Acts 26:20 that we "should repent and turn to God, *performing deeds appropriate to repentance*"? This change of mind also involves his will cooperating with his mind or else he was not really convinced. Why else would the Bible require the fruit of obedience to God as the necessary

---

[1]Incredibly, Zane Hodges denies that "life" here is "eternal life" even though the reason for Peter's words was that the Gentile house of Cornelius had been converted: *Absolutely Free!* (Grand Rapids: Zondervan, 1989), p. 153. See however Acts 2:28; 3:15; 13:46, 48. Of course Hodges finds some "distinctions" in Acts 11:18, based on a "literal" hermeneutic, of course. I must say that Hodges' book is full of such twistings, and like Dillow, when his point is the weakest he uses many exclamation points.

evidence of repentance if the will had no place? What would we think of John Doe who said he had reconsidered marrying Jane Jones, but he married her? Would you not correctly conclude that he had not really changed his mind about her?

When we say repentance is turning from sin, Dillow thinks we mean that God looks for obedience *before* He forgives the sinner. To him "turning" is obedience rather than a mental recognition of our sins as odious to God that results in obedience. Typically, Dillow misunderstands the Reformed, as well as the Bible, which specifically commands us to "turn from our sins." Likewise Ryrie reveals the same misunderstanding when he blunders: "Is repentance a condition for receiving eternal life? Yes, if it is . . . changing one's mind about Jesus Christ. No, if it means to be sorry for sin or even to resolve to turn from sin, for these things *will not save*" [emphasis his].[2] As Kenneth Gentry rightly observes, Ryrie's view of repentance disregards sin, the very reason one comes to Jesus.[3] One simply changes his mind about Jesus but not about his sin, which leads us to ask, Why go to Jesus? If one does not go to Jesus because he has changed his mind about his sin, then he is not believing the Gospel. He would not be going to Jesus to have his sins forgiven but for some kind of gift that had nothing to do with sin.

Of course it is true that "these things will not save." Whoever said they would? Faith does not save either, only Jesus does. Faith/repentance is the *sole instrument* through which God saves, the *sole cause* is the grace of God, especially in His electing grace, the *sole ground* is Jesus' life, death, and resurrection, and the *fruit* is good works. Thus we are justified by faith alone in Jesus alone, by God's grace alone, and to His glory alone.

Roy B. Zuck, who also has taught at DTS, said, "Repentance is included in believing. Faith and repentance are like two sides of a coin. Genuine faith includes repentance, and genuine repentance includes faith. . . . Repentance is a turn-

---

[2]Charles Ryrie, *So Great Salvation* (Victor Books, 1989), p. 99; likewise J. Dwight Pentecost, *Things Which Become Sound Doctrine* (Grand Rapids: Zondervan, 1965), p. 61ff.

[3]Kenneth L. Gentry, Jr., *Lord of the Saved* (Phillipsburg: Presbyterian and Reformed, 1992), p. 42.

ing *from* sin, while faith is turning *to* Christ. A change of outlook toward both sin and Christ, as Lewis Sperry Chafer has noted, 'promises a change in the course being pursued'" [emphasis his].[4] Notice that Zuck and Ryrie disagree, that no Reformed theologian would disagree with Zuck's analysis, though he thinks he is saying something different from the Reformed, and that if a "change in the course pursued" is inherent in repentance, then we have lordship salvation.

Zuck seems to indicate in his article that though "some fruit" or some change will happen to all Christians who have the Spirit, it is not a necessary change. If you can make sense out of that contradiction, you need help. Sometimes antinomians say that though surrender may be included in faith, it must not be made an explicit condition. Surrender is, they say, a separate issue, so do not make it a "condition" for receiving the free gift of eternal life; do not tell sinners that they must give up anything when coming to Jesus. In other words, it is legitimate to surrender to Jesus as long as one does not know he is doing it and does not do it initially. Let the sinner have the free gift, then only later let him know he has not been told the whole story. This is what would seem to be a salesman's gimmick, bait and switch, in contrast to the Lord who told people up front and honestly to count the cost.

Zuck has given a good understanding of repentance but then he says: ". . . if someone says a person must commit, surrender, obey, forsake all, or deny self in order to receive that gift and be saved, that implies that salvation is not a gift after all."[5] In other words, a sinner must change his mind about his sin and Jesus but not "commit, surrender, obey. . . ." Zuck is hopelessly confused. On the one hand, what Reformed theologian ever said that to "obey" is a condition of the Gospel? Of course, he does not quote one.[6] On the other hand, the Lord God incarnate Himself proclaimed that one must "hate his father and mother, wife and children, brothers

---

[4]*Kindred Spirit* magazine, Summer 1989, p. 5, published by DTS.

[5]Ibid.

[6]By the way, I have never seen Ryrie, Hodges, Pentecost, Dillow or any one document their understanding that the Reformed are saying that repentance is obedience and is a pre-condition to justification. This is a straw man and thus cannot be documented.

and sisters, yes, and his own life also" (Luke 14:26), which is another way of saying that we must "surrender, forsake, and deny" our sins. This is not the same as obeying; the Lord's statement commands repentance and obedience is the fruit of repentance. Typically, Zuck has mixed terms.

Furthermore, there is no neutrality. What attitude should a person have who comes to Jesus for forgiveness of sins? Should he love his sins, or is this just not an issue? If it is not an issue, then repentance is not a change of mind about one's sins, God, and Christ. Zuck would have a sinner change his mind about his sins, come to Jesus and say, "I want eternal life but don't ask me about my sins; this is a separate issue." Or, "I have changed my mind about my sins, Jesus, and I now hate them, but don't ask me to forsake them." How can one quit loving his sins and not forsake them, change his mind about them and not surrender his whole life to Jesus? This assumes some sort of neutrality and that the reason for going to Jesus is something other than one's sins. The Lord does not give one eternal life apart from dealing with one's sins, for eternal life is about sin: "For the wages of sin is death, but the gift of God is eternal life in Christ Jesus our Lord" (Rom. 6:23).

Like faith, repentance is a mental understanding, and also an agreement with that understanding which reveals its validity in obedience. Repentance is not obedience but results in obedience. Obviously God knows immediately if the repentance is genuine or not, and He forgives the person if the repentance is real. The obedience reveals the validity of faith/repentance, demonstrating that the initial faith/repentance was genuine and further repentance shows that God "continues the work He has begun" (Phil. 1:6) in the saint. If one truly repents, he recognizes his sins, is sorry for them (2 Cor. 7:8-10)[7] — not because he was caught but because they are an offense to God — hates his sins, knows he cannot justify himself, sees God's mercy in Christ and embraces Jesus as his

---

[7] Because "godly sorrow" is mentioned separately from repentance in 2 Corinthians 7:8-10, some say that it is not part of repentance. But if godly sorrow — sorrow over our sin produced by God — invariably leads to repentance, then the two must be tied together. They are not identical, but one cannot exist without the other. It is again the hermeneutic of distinctions and the idea that God's truths are like unstrung beads on a floor that lead some to such a conclusion.

Lord and Savior. This is not works. The person may not consciously think of each one of these points, but in some form they are present. Scripture recognizes a false repentance in Cain, Esau, and Judas, who were sorry over the consequences of their sins to themselves, but not over the offensiveness of their sins to God.[8]

In neither repentance (negative: a turning from) nor faith (positive: turning to) is its nature only an understanding without assenting to that understanding and embracing Christ with the will. Most Reformed theologians consider trusting as separate from assenting, while Reformed theologian Gordon Clark considers it and assent as the same, but all the Reformed state that repentance necessarily issues in a corresponding change of life. If one does not have the fruit, then he does not have the root; he is still dead in his sins.

The nature of repentance also entails that the sinner is aware of his lost condition because he has broken God's law: "For by the law comes the knowledge of sin" (Rom. 3:20). The WCF summarizes the concept with great precision:

> By it, a sinner, out of the sight and sense not only of the danger, but also of the filthiness and odiousness of his sins, as contrary to the holy nature, and righteous law of God; and upon the apprehension of His mercy in Christ to such as are penitent, so grieves for, and hates his sins, as to turn from them all unto God, purposing and endeavoring to walk with Him in all the ways of His commandments.

In repentance one purposes to walk with Him, but the actual walking is the fruit. In faith one trusts Jesus as Lord, but the actual obedience is the fruit.

Today's Christian culture is satiated with the false notion that God is standing by begging people to *let* Him save them, to relieve His anxiety so He can give them some gift. This is emphatically not true; rather, the Gospel is that man is a sinner, under the wrath of Almighty God, and on his way to hell (Rom. 1:18-3:20). He is completely deserving of this judgment, totally without righteousness, totally incapable of pleasing Him. Jesus is the only Savior from this judgment

---

[8]False repentance is sometimes recognized by the Greek *metamelomai* as opposed to *metanoeo*, which is usually genuine repentance.

and hell, and He gives righteousness to the one who will confess his sins, turn away from all his sins to Jesus, and cast himself solely on the mercy of Jesus (Rom. 3:21-4:11). It is not that he can do God a favor, but that God *commands* him to repent and believe the Gospel under the penalty of eternal hell.

A stunning example of true conversion is in Luke 18:9ff, where the penitent sinner would not even look up toward heaven, realizing what a miserable sinner he was, "kept smiting"[9] his breast (repentance), and said, "God be merciful to me the sinner" (faith). The Greek indicates that he asked for mercy on the basis of sacrifice (*hilastheti*), the death of a substitute, pointing to Jesus. He did not ask for a gift and love his sins; the Pharisee did that, thanking God as to how good he was, pleased with himself and his pride. Jesus' statement is a fitting conclusion: "I tell you, this man went down to his house justified rather than the other [Pharisee]; for everyone who exalts himself will be abased, and he who humbles himself will be exalted" (v. 14). Abasing oneself is repentance; exalting oneself is pride, arrogance, and antinomianism. Sin is the issue; Jesus is the solution. Are we to think that the penitent sinner surrendered himself to God to have his sins forgiven but did not surrender his sins, especially his pride? If he asked forgiveness for something he did not surrender, then he did not really ask sincerely, for he would be asking for forgiveness so he could keep on sinning.

It is imperative to preach repentance. Our Lord preached it, and He commanded the Apostles to preach it beginning at Jerusalem (Luke 24:46, 47). Peter preached it to the Jews (Acts 2:38; 2 Peter 3:9), and Paul to the Gentiles (Acts 20:21; 26:18-20; 2 Cor. 7:8-10; 2 Tim. 2:25). Thus repentance is a vital part of Christ's Gospel in the Great Commission, and to omit it is to disgrace and change the Gospel of grace. To omit preaching it would be tantamount to preaching a Gospel without preaching about sin and the need for the Gospel. Too often this is what is done, for God is presented as the friend of every man and man as able to relieve God's stress over wanting to save those who will not let Him. Allegedly man can believe at any time, and God is wringing His hands.

---

[9] So the Greek imperfect tense should be rendered in this case.

Rather, God is every man's enemy (Rom. 5:10), and the truth is that God will relieve man's stress over breaking His laws. The issue is man's sins and the broken law of God, not God's love and broken heart. God has no needs, especially no broken heart, and man cannot even repent and believe; he is totally at the mercy of God. God is not in trouble, man is. It is not man who can do God a favor, but God who can do man a favor. Man is under the wrath of God and on his way to hell because of his sins (Rom. 1:18ff), and he had better recognize this (repent) and embrace Jesus (faith).

To preach repentance one must proclaim the law of God to show natural man his need of Jesus, and then preach the law to direct the justified man to the path of obedience. To omit these two uses of God's holy law breeds an antinomian dislike for God's commands, a license that blasphemes God's grace by implying that God saves His people with the option of living in sin. Today's Christian culture basically despises God's law. We are too interested in showing man how God can help him, and not concerned in being like Paul who exposed man's need of the Savior by God's law (Rom. 1:18-3:20). Robert Shaw, a Reformed theologian from last century, is enlightening on this point:

> To cover our sins is to dishonor God, as if he either did not see, or could not punish them; whereas, to confess our sins is to honor God's holy law, which we have violated — to honor his omniscience, which beheld all our transgressions — to honor his patience and long-suffering, which have forborne to execute the merited punishment.[10]

Often we make it too easy for one to become a Christian. We tell him all he has to do is trust Christ as sin bearer and imply (if we do not tell him explicitly) that he may serve two masters if he so wishes. We do not tell him to count the cost. Yet the Lord incarnate did not agree with our method; for He understood the nature of repentance as more than a simple change of understanding without assenting to the change:

---

[10]Robert Shaw, *The Reformed Faith* (Inverness, Scotland: Christian Focus Publications, 1845, 1974), p. 160.

If anyone *comes to Me*,[11] and does not hate his own father and mother and wife and children and brothers and sisters, yes, and even his own life, he cannot be My disciple. For . . . first sit down and calculate the cost . . . (Luke 14:26-28).

It is true that we must trust Christ as sin bearer, and this is sufficient if we understand trust biblically. Therefore, since many do not preach repentance, our churches are full of "carnal" Christians who are nothing more than self-satisfied hypocrites who try to run the churches (and often do) by the natural mind. Their destiny is the lake of fire. Those who gave them a half Gospel will be judged also.

Or they bellow, "How many sins must one turn from before he is assured of justification?" They think that the challenge to define how many sins nullifies God's specific command to turn from them. It is the same kind of question the hypocrite asked Christ when the Lord told him to love his neighbor as himself. The man thought he could circumnavigate the impact of Jesus' penetrating statement by asking a question of definition: "But wishing to justify himself, he said to Jesus, 'And who is my neighbor'?" (Luke 10:29). By the pungent story of the Good Samaritan, the Lord said one's neighbor is everyone. Likewise the antinomians hope to avoid repentance by asking a defining question: How many sins must one turn from? The Lord's answer is succinct: "Deny *yourself*, and follow Me."

What Repentance Is Not

Now that we have seen what repentance is, caution should be taken to notice what repentance is not. For instance, it is not penance, not a good work done to merit forgiveness. People often confuse the fruit with the root. Repentance arises from a good heart, one created by God; it does not create the good heart.

God does not require perfect obedience (or any obedience) of the sinner before He forgives. Obedience flows from

---

[11]The expression "comes to Me" is used of coming to Christ for salvation in the Gospels, not simply for discipleship, as if the two were separate: used here; see also Luke 6:47ff; 9:23ff; John 6:35. The Greek respectively is: τις ερχεται προς με; πας ο ερχομενος προς με; ει τις θελει οπισω μου ελθειν; ο ερχομενος προς με.

repentance and faith; it is not meritorious either before or after faith. We would not say that faith *is* obedience but that faith *produces* obedience. When one believes in Jesus, God does not consider the works inherent in faith in justifying the sinner; He only considers the faith. Repentance — like faith — is both initial and continual. By initial repentance the sinner is forgiven, and by continual repentance his life is one of habitually turning from his sins to Christ. Repentance is a deep rooted change within the heart that arises from regeneration and manifests itself by its fruits.

Also repentance is not the *basis* for pardon; it is only the *means*.

> True repentance and pardon are inseparably connected. Though no one is pardoned for his repentance, yet repentance is of such indispensable necessity, that an impenitent sinner cannot be a pardoned sinner. They are connected in the economy of salvation, not as cause and effect, but to show the consistency of a gratuitous pardon with the interests of holiness.[12]

Repentance is not confession to a human priest for forgiveness, but to the Lord Christ alone who is the sole mediator between God and man (1 Tim. 2:5).

And finally, repentance is not worked up by man, but is God's gift to His elect (Acts 5:31; 11:18; 2 Tim. 2:25; Jer. 31:18, 19). No man is able of himself either to repent or believe (John 6:44, 45, 65; Isa. 64:6, 7; Rom. 8:7, 8; 1 Cor. 2:14), thus God must effectually work repentance in the hearts of His own or they will never have it.

Is Repentance in John?

Dillow confidently asserts that John's Gospel never requires repentance to receive eternal life, but that John did state that one becomes a Christian by reading and believing his Gospel. The conclusion Dillow reaches is that repentance is not necessary for justification. It is true that John never specifically mentions repentance by name and that John wrote the Gospel so that readers could have life (John 20:30, 31). Again, however, Dillow has misunderstood the Reformed Faith and

---

[12]Robert Shaw, *The Reformed Faith*, p. 158

the Bible. Both the Bible and the Reformed state that true faith is impossible without repentance, which is why only faith is mentioned in some passages, only repentance in others, and yet both in different contexts (see below).

Furthermore, Dillow commits two logical fallacies: Because the term repentance is not mentioned in John does not mean the idea is not present, and the absence of the idea in one part of Scripture cannot negate its presence in another section of the Bible. An example of the former is an argument the Jehovah's Witnesses use when they say the term "Trinity" is not found in the Bible, but the orthodox have responded that the idea is there. An example of the latter is that a thief cannot negate the bad act of stealing by other good acts. Likewise, the presence of repentance, especially in most of the sermons the Apostles preached in Acts, cannot be deafened by its silence in John.

John, however, does speak of repentance. He proclaims that the reason some will not come to Christ is that they love the darkness or their sin (John 3:19-21), that His sheep follow Him (John 10:26-28), that we must hate our lives to gain eternal life (John 12:24-26), and especially that the Holy Spirit convicts us of sin and the judgment to come (John 16:8-11).

In John 8 the Lord rebuked those who had just believed in Him (John 8:30) that they were truly His only if they endured (v. 31), and He indicts them of numerous sins, because they did not believe that they were sinners (v. 33). He says they are guilty of not having His Word in them (v. 37), not listening to Him (vv. 40-43), being of the devil (v. 44), not believing Him (vv. 45, 46) and being liars (v. 55). The Lord is teaching that it is "the sick who need the physician" while "those who are well" will not come to the Great Physician. In other words, without repentance from one's personal sins, without recognizing that one is personally a sinner, he will not come to the Son who makes free. In no uncertain terms, the Lord refused to recognize their profession of faith as genuine because they had not repented. They could not have Him as Savior without also recognizing their sins, for the precise reason that believing in Him was a personal sin question. Repentance *is* in John, therefore, though the word is not used.

Likewise, in Acts 2:23; 3:13; 5:30, Peter accused the Jews of murdering the Messiah which of course was done in unbelief, but it was still a personal sin. Peter preached against both unbelief and their specific sins. At Ephesus Paul's preaching led to the converts burning their books (Acts 19:19), which was done because they "believed, came confessing and telling their deeds" (v. 18). Preaching the Gospel necessitates preaching against the sins of the day, and in Romans 1:18ff Paul preached against homosexuality, lying, unthankfulness, and so forth.

In Luke 24:46-47 we read: "Then He said to them, 'Thus it is written, and thus it was necessary for the Christ to suffer and to rise from the dead the third day, and that *repentance* and remission of sins should be preached in His name to all nations [Gentiles must repent], beginning at Jerusalem.'" In Acts 1:8 Luke does not mention either faith or repentance, and yet he quotes the Lord who commands His Apostles to take the Gospel to all the nations, which would include Gentiles. In Mark 16:15, 16 the Lord said to take the Gospel to all the world and the one who *believes* will be justified. If Luke only mentions repentance in his Great Commission, does this mean faith is not necessary? If Mark only mentions belief, is repentance not necessary? Who has the right Gospel, John, Luke, or Mark? The obvious answer is that all of them do. We do not use the disparity method of interpreting (by pitting one passage against another) that Dillow promotes, but by the analogy of Scripture we understand that faith and repentance are not mutually exclusive; but one implies the other.

What Is Faith?

Hardly anyone would doubt the necessity of faith in Jesus for forgiveness of sins. Notice what Scripture says:

> He who believes in the Son has everlasting life; and he who does not obey the Son shall not see life, but the wrath of God abides on him (John 3:36).

> So they said, "Believe on the Lord Jesus Christ, and you will be saved, you and your household" (Acts 16:31).

Knowing that a man is not justified by the works of the law
but through faith in Christ Jesus (Gal. 2:16).

The Bible is emphatic that one must trust only in the Lord
Christ for acceptance with God. The WCF summarizes faith
well from Scripture as an "accepting, receiving, and resting
upon Christ alone for justification, sanctification, and eternal
life."[13]

But what specifically is the nature of saving faith? What
constitutes genuine faith as opposed to a spurious faith? Zane
Hodges is very "instructive" in his definition of saving faith:
"The word 'believe' means 'believe' — both in English and in
Greek."[14] Such nonsense does not deserve an answer, for one
cannot define a word by repeating it.

Faith Includes the Whole Man

How can one discern if his faith is veritable or if he is
self-deceived? If one can be self-deceived as Dillow allows, and
if false teachers abound (2 Cor. 11; 2 Peter 2; 1 John 4:1-6),
how are we to distinguish the true from the false? Are the
tests only propositions about Jesus or do they include moral
tests as well? If one reads the verses in parentheses just cited,
he will find both kinds of tests, objective and subjective.
Furthermore, Protestants have generally considered three
elements to be necessary to saving faith. The first element is
knowledge (*notitia*) about God, himself, and especially about
Christ. The second and third elements are assent (*assensus*) to
that knowledge and trust (*fiducia*) or personal commitment
to the assent and knowledge. Since this is not an exhaustive
treatment, we shall consider these three together.

In Titus 1:16 Paul proclaims: "They profess to know God,
but by [their] deeds they deny [Him], being detestable and
disobedient." Paul does not say that they have the wrong
propositions (though this could also invalidate one's profession — 1 John 4:1-6) but that their deeds invalidated their
claim. Consequently, one can have the right content (be
intellectually correct), but not have true faith if his profession

---

[13] We observe that it is by faith that we are sanctified — not by our works, as
Dillow would say.

[14] Hodges, *Absolutely Free*, p. 145.

does not involve the will in bowing to God and His Word. Therefore, one who claims to know Christ as Savior but does not bow to Him as Lord is deceiving himself. He has the kind of faith James says the demons have (2:14ff), which is a knowledge of Him without obedience. Such professors — and that is all they are — deceive themselves into hell. Genuine faith necessarily manifests itself by obedience; otherwise it is a veneer, only skin deep, a facade. The sinner trusts in the *whole* Christ with his *whole* soul, mind, will, and affections. The Puritan divine, John Flavel (1628-1691), expressed it very well in his writings:

> Christ is offered to us in the Gospel entirely and undividedly, as clothed with all his offices, priestly, prophetical, and regal; as Christ Jesus the Lord, Acts 16:31, and so the true believer receives him; the hypocrite, like the harlot, is for dividing, but the sincere believer finds the need he hath of every office of Christ, and knows not how to want [give up] any thing that is in him.

> His ignorance makes him necessary and desirable to him as a PROPHET: His guilt makes him necessary as a PRIEST: His strong and powerful lusts and corruptions make him necessary as a KING: and in truth, he sees not anything in Christ he can spare; he needs all that is Christ, and admires infinite wisdom in nothing more than the investing Christ with all these offices, which are so suited to the poor sinner's wants [defects] and miseries. Look, as the three offices are undivided in Christ, so they are in the believer's acceptance; and before this trial no hypocrite can stand; for all hypocrites reject and quarrel with something in Christ; they like his pardon better than his government. They call him indeed, Lord and Master, but it is an empty title they bestow upon him; for let them ask their own hearts if Christ be Lord over their thoughts, as well as words; over their secret as well as open actions; over their darling lusts, as well as others; let them ask, who will appear to be Lord and Master over them, when Christ and the world come in competition? When the pleasure of sin shall stand upon one side, and sufferings to death, and deepest points of self-denial upon the other side? Surely it is the greatest affront that can be offered to the Divine Wisdom and Goodness, to

separate in our acceptance, what is so united in Christ, for our salvation and happiness. As without any one of these offices, the work of salvation could not be completed, so without acceptance of Christ in them all, our union with him by faith cannot be completed.

The Gospel offer of Christ includes all his offices, and Gospel faith just so receives him; to submit to him, as well as be redeemed by him; to imitate him in the holiness of his life, as well as to reap the purchases and fruits of his death. It must be an entire receiving of the Lord Jesus Christ.[15]

Dillow advocates dividing Christ and looking to Him as priest but not as king. "One can know Him as savior while not knowing Him as Lord," he maintains. Thus, part of man — his intellect — looks to part of Christ — His priesthood. What a travesty to God's grace. Christ came to save His people *from* their sins — not *in* their sins (Matt. 1:21). Dillow would hold primarily to faith as understanding or knowledge and perhaps to some form of assent, but he denies that the will is involved in saving faith. And as Robert Shaw so accurately states:

Romanists make faith to be nothing more than a bare naked assent to the truth revealed in the Word. This notion was strenuously opposed by our Reformers, and is renounced in the National Covenant of Scotland, under the name of a "general and doubtsome faith"; yet, many Protestants, in modern times, represent saving faith as nothing more than a simple assent to the doctrinal truths recorded in Scripture, and as exclusively an act of the understanding.[16]

James 2 legislates that faith without works is dead. Zane Hodges agrees but says the person is still a Christian.[17] Dillow agrees with this (p. 188). Dillow and Hodges present us with a person who has no faith but is still justified, and Hodges accuses those who reject his position of being of the devil![18]

---

[15] *Works of John Flavel*, (London: The Banner of Truth Trust, 1968), 2:110-111.

[16] Shaw, Op Cit., p. 149.

[17] Zane Hodges, *The Gospel Under Siege* (Dallas: Redencion Viva, date early 1970's), pp. 20, 33.

[18] Ibid., p. 6.

His concept of faith is mental acknowledgement without the will, the exact thing James says the demons have. He is not able to see that faith necessarily contains works (Eph. 2:10). To Mr. Hodges and others like him, if we say that works are necessary at any point, then we have corrupted the Gospel. They are not able to see that works are united in faith but are not what God views in justifying the sinner. As Dr. John Gerstner so ably states, *"From the essential truth that no sinner in himself can merit salvation, the antinomian draws the erroneous conclusion that good works need not even accompany faith in the saint.* The question is not whether good works are necessary to salvation, but in what way are they necessary. As the inevitable outworking of saving faith, they are necessary for salvation. As the meritorious ground of justification, they are not necessary *or acceptable"* [emphasis his].[19]

Faith Excludes Implicit Knowledge

We agree with Hodges and Dillow that faith includes the understanding, but contrary to them it is not this only. Calvin also in his *Institutes* solemnly pronounces that faith without understanding is not faith. Calvin and the Reformers opposed the Roman Catholic doctrine of "implicit faith." Implicit faith was supposedly faith without knowledge, as one may see in this hypothetical dialogue: "What do you believe?" Response: "I believe whatever the Roman Catholic Church believes." Elaboration: "What does the church believe?" Response: "I don't know what all it believes, but I believe it." We agree with Dillow that true faith must have accurate knowledge, but this does not exhaust saving faith.

Dillow says that ". . . faith itself is not a volitional but a mental act. . . ." (p. 282). He quotes Warfield approvingly: "It is impossible that belief should be the product of a voli-tion. . . ." (p. 278). What he missed is that Warfield means that faith does not *arise* from merely an arbitrary act of the will; it arises from true knowledge of God and of Christ. One cannot believe what his mind tells him is false or what he does not know. In existentialism one believes what he knows is false so that faith is a leap into the dark, and Warfield denies such.

---

[19]John H. Gerstner, *Wrongly Dividing the Word of Truth* (Brentwood, TN: Wolgemuth & Hyatt, 1991), p. 210.

Warfield's entire article *emphasizes* true knowledge but does not *eliminate* the will, and Dillow has typically misquoted him.

In our anti-intellectual day when people want to "experience" God instead of knowing Him through the propositions of Scripture, the emphasis that faith is assent to understood propositions needs to be proclaimed from the roof tops. We live in the day of existentialism when seminary students are taught that theology is dry and that we need to "encounter" God. Consequently when they enter the pulpits, they do not preach doctrine but "coming forward" for experiences. After all, they say no one can figure out the Bible, we should not worry about doctrine, and there is no creed but Christ.

If we may further emphasize true knowledge to those who say they have no creed but Christ, we would ask, Which Christ does the preacher present: the Jesus of Mormonism, of the Jehovah's Witnesses, of Christian Science, or of the Bible? The Jesus of the cults does not exist, and all "faith" in him is void. One's faith is only as good as the object, and the object only as reliable as the propositions about the object. Most people in the pews do not want "dry" doctrine; they want nice stories and illustrations. But the God of the Bible has revealed Himself in a Book that has many propositions about Himself, and believing *that* something is true about God is just as important as believing *in* Him. It is quite impossible to believe in Him without believing facts that reveal Him. The point, therefore, that faith must have knowledge to be genuine is a much needed emphasis, and we hope that this continues.[20]

---

[20]William G. T. Shedd in *Dogmatic Theology*, volume 2, about page 500, makes a distinction between believing *in* or *on* Christ and believing *that* something is true about Christ. While it may be possible to theorize such a distinction ("We believe *that* Johnny has blue eyes, but we do not believe *in* Johnny"), the New Testament does not seem to confirm this grammatically. Especially in John's Gospel, believing *in* Christ and believing *that* Jesus is the Son of God are not different. In other words, believing a proposition *about* Christ is often believing *in* Him. We are not denying the New Testament distinction between assent and trust, but only that the strict grammar of believing *in* and believing *that* are not different, for one can believe *in* Jesus and not have trust (John 8:30ff) and one can believe *that* He is the Son of God and have trust in Him (John 20:31). We do not deny that usually believing *in* or *on* is stronger than simply believing without the preposition (simple dative). See the grammars: F. Blass and A. DeBrunner, *A Greek Grammar of the New Testament and Other Early Christian Literature* (Chicago: The University of Chicago Press, 1970), #187(6), 235(2),

Sometimes what preachers mean by "no creed but Christ" is that Jesus Himself, not simply doctrine abstractly considered, is the object of faith, and this is of course true. Jesus is greater than His revelation of Himself to us. However, though one can embrace doctrine without embracing Jesus, he cannot embrace Jesus without embracing the correct doctrine.

Believing propositions does not preclude that the will is not involved. Warfield, in the same article, discusses the three elements of faith as knowledge (*notitia*), assent (*assensus*), and trust or commitment (*fiducia*).[21] Again Warfield states: "The central movement in all faith is no doubt the element of assent. . . ."[22] Warfield explains: "In every movement of faith, therefore, from the lowest to the highest, there is an intellectual, an emotional, *and a voluntary element*" [emphasis added].[23] Warfield says that the "movement of assent must depend . . . not specifically [on] the will, but [on] the intellect. . . " by which he means, contrary to Roman Catholicism, that one must have intelligent faith. He emphatically does not mean that true faith has no volitional element in it, for the "voluntary element" is volitional. In another article in the same book, Warfield explains James 2:

> It is not faith as he [James] conceives it which he deprecates, but that professed faith which cannot be shown to be real by appropriate works. . . . In short, James is not depreciating faith: with him, too, it is faith that is reckoned unto righteousness (2:23), though only such faith as shows itself in works can be so reckoned, because a faith which does not come to

---

397(2); A. T. Robertson, *A Grammar of the Greek New Testament in the Light of Historical Research* (Nashville: Broadman Press, 1934), pp. 453, 476, *540*; and especially James Hope Moulton, *A Grammar of New Testament Greek: Prolegomena* (Edinburgh: T. & T. Clark, 1967), p. 61ff. Moulton argues that believing *in* is trust and *believe* without a preposition means simple belief while Blass disagrees. See also C. F. D. Moule, *An Idiom-Book of New Testament Greek* (Cambridge: University Press, 1971), pp. 69, 80, and Ernest DeWitt Burton, *International Critical Commentary: A Critical and Exegetical Commentary on the Epistle to the Galatians* (Edinburgh: T. & T. Clark, 1971), p. 477ff.

[21] B. B. Warfield, *Biblical and Theological Studies* (Philadelphia: Presbyterian and Reformed, 1952), p. 402.

[22] Ibid., p. 403.

[23] Ibid.

fruitage in works is dead, non-existent. He is rather deepening the idea of faith, and insisting *that it includes in its very conception something more than an otiose* [idle, empty] *intellectual assent* [emphasis added].[24]

Dillow, contrary to Warfield, vehemently maintains that faith is correct knowledge without the will involved. But what Dillow misses is that even true *knowledge* of Christ is effectual and inevitably produces fruit:

> By this we know that we have come to know Him, if we keep His commandments. The one who says, "I have come to know Him," and does not keep His commandments, is a liar, and the truth is not in him (1 John 2:3, 4).

According to John, if one has true knowledge of Jesus, his life is so changed that he will keep God's commands. Saving knowledge of Jesus is not simply a mental understanding.

Faith and Gordon Clark

Dillow and especially Hodges quote Gordon Clark as supporting their position. In fact, Gordon Clark, who is very exacting in defining faith in *Faith and Saving Faith*, challenges such heavyweights as Thomas Manton, John Owen, Charles Hodge, Warfield, and others for considering that faith is more than assent to understood propositions.[25] Dillow and Hodges, however, have either misunderstood Clark or misrepresented him, for even though Clark may not be within the mainstream of the Reformed tradition on this point, he still maintains that assent is volitional,[26] and strongly con-

---

[24]Ibid., p. 416.

[25]This sounds very close to Sandemanianism after Robert Sandeman (1718-71) who "held that bare assent to the work of Christ is" saving faith, J. D. Douglas, *The New International Dictionary of the Christian Church* (Grand Rapids: Zondervan, 1974), p. 877. See also Kenneth Scott Latourette, *Christianity in a Revolutionary Age: Vol. 2: The 19th Century in Europe* (Grand Rapids: Zondervan, 1976), pp. 386, 422-23; A. A. Hodge, *Outlines of Theology* (Grand Rapids: Zondervan, 1976), p. 472; and especially John MacLeod, *Scottish Theology* (Carlisle, PA: The Banner of Truth Trust, 1974), p. 185ff. However, because Clark connects works to faith as the necessary effect, it would seem that he avoids Sandemanianism.

[26]Gordon Clark, *Faith and Saving Faith*, p. 65. See also Gordon Clark, *The Johannine Logos* (Phillipsburgh: Presbyterian & Reformed, 1972), especially

tends that true faith produces works, both of which Hodges and Dillow deny.

Furthermore, Gordon Clark, in *Faith and Saving Faith*, approvingly quotes Calvin's *Institutes* and Machen in *What Is Faith?*[27] maintaining that assenting intellectually to something is believing it. He views all faith the same, whether held by the atheist in his beliefs or the Christian in Christ, and that faith involves only two aspects: knowledge and assenting to that knowledge. It appears that Clark does not distinguish trust and assenting, considering them to be the same.

Most Reformed theologians do not agree with Clark. Though Clark attempts to explain the demons in James 2, he does not seem to do justice regarding these demons who believe right facts about God, assent to these facts, but are not converted.[28] It would seem that the demons know and assent to the whole plan of salvation, which is why they oppose Christians and their Gospel so vehemently. Satan blinds the minds of the unregenerate so that they do not receive the Gospel, which would seem to indicate that he understands and assents to the power of the Gospel or else what would he blind them to? Why and how could Satan clone the Gospel if he did not fear it and assent to its power? Contrary to Clark, James is discussing the nature of faith as seen by the terms used: "faith by itself" (v. 17), "faith without works is dead" (vv. 20, 26), the demons do well to believe in one God (v. 19). James does not say that more or different knowledge is what is needed but a different kind of faith — one that produces works.

It is difficult to follow Clark who seems to say it is

---

chapter 5, "Saving Faith."

[27]Machen does speak of trust in faith, *What Is Faith?*, p. 143. I highly recommend reading this very relevant work for the same heresies are troubling "Israel" again.

[28]Clark would say that the demons were monotheists only, which meant that they did not believe enough right propositions (*Johannine Logos*, p. 81). But it seems to me that James is discussing kinds of faith, not propositions, so that the difference is qualitative, not quantitative. For an elaboration of Satan's knowledge and of the nature of saving faith, see *The Works of Jonathan Edwards* (Carlisle, PA: The Banner of Truth Trust, 1976), "True Grace Distinguished from the Experience of Devils," p. 41ff. See also "Concerning Faith" on p. 578ff. Must reading!

theoretically impossible for anyone to know the Gospel facts, acknowledge them as true, and not be a Christian. This would tend to make ignorance the primary sin instead of disobedience.[29] In Romans 1 Paul says of the ungodly that they know God yet they suppress the truth because they do not *want* the Gospel and because they *love* their sin (1:18ff; see also John 3:19-21). The problem is not so much knowledge as it is hatred of knowledge. The Lord told His disciples to do what the scribes said but not what they did (Matt. 23:3), indicating that they had the right knowledge but not the right practice, and I'm sure the scribes proclaimed that they had the truth and assented to it.

In the Gospels the demons proclaimed that Jesus was the Son of God (Matt. 8:29, etc.), revealing that they had right knowledge and assented to it, but they were not converted; they did not trust in Jesus. In 1 John 4:15 confessing Jesus as the Son of God means one is a Christian. The knowledge and assent of the demons and the Christians are the same, and as Jonathan Edwards argues, the difference has to be in the nature of faith.[30] In fact, neither the demons nor the devil ever hesitated to obey the Lord's word when He commanded them to do something, revealing that they both knew Him and assented to Him. Perhaps the demons and Satan did not know everything about the plan of redemption (1 Cor. 2:8), but neither do most people when they are converted.

In Matthew 13 in the parable of the sower, there were some who received the word with joy and yet fell away. They had knowledge, assented to it, and yet were not Christians. Did they have joy in their ignorance or without assenting? This is not what the Lord says, though the true Christians understood more fully (Matt. 13:13, 19, 23).

In John 8:31 John specifically states that some Jews "had believed in" Jesus, yet later the Lord declares they are of their

---

[29]Ignorance is sin (Hosea 4:6), but primarily sin is disobedience. The one who ignorantly disobeys will be judged, but the one who willfully disobeys will be judged more severely (Luke 12:47-48). Gnostics hold that the nature of sin is ignorance while evangelicals say that it is rebellion. With the former sin is epistemological while with the latter it is ethical. Clark, who died about eight years ago, was certainly not gnostic.

[30]See Op. Cit.

father the devil (v. 44), indicating that their belief was void. And it was void because they did not continue in His Word (v. 31) and because they did not really believe the right things about Jesus (vv. 32, 45-46). Both the nature of their faith and the propositions believed were false.

One other example comes to mind. When Peter did a mighty miracle by the power of Jesus, the rulers said "We cannot deny it" (Acts 4:16). They had knowledge, assented to it, and still rejected Christ.

In these examples Clark's response would probably be that they did not really assent to the knowledge they had or else they did not assent to enough propositions to be truly justified, but this does not seem to be what the texts say.[31]

What is the Relationship of Faith to Repentance?

Often in Scripture repentance is the only requirement for justification, and yet faith is the sole prerequisite in other passages; and further still, sometimes both are necessary (Mark 1:15; Acts 20:21). How can this be? How can God require faith at one time, repentance at another, and at a third time both? The answer is that the two concepts fall or stand together; they imply one another.

Both Produce Works

The first point of unity between repentance and faith is that both have the same necessary fruit: good works. Even as works

---

[31]With Clark it is never the nature of faith that is in question, for all faith (the atheist in his belief and the Christian in his faith) has the same nature: assent to propositions intellectually comprehended. Though I have disagreed with Clark to some extent, both Clark and most of the other Reformed men end up at the same place regarding our topic: saving faith includes the will and has good works as its effect. Clark's problem may be a defective view of knowledge, see the critique of him regarding James 2 in R. C. Sproul, *Classical Apologetics* (Grand Rapids: Zondervan, 1984), p. 333ff. Jonathan Edwards regarded saving faith as supernatural (see Op. Cit.) while Clark sees saving faith and the faith of the atheist as the same in nature, which involves a certain view of being, knowledge, psychology of man, etc., which does not seem to be correct, though I am personally in Clark's camp in apologetics and more so in Van Til's. For more on this see Cornelius Van Til's *The Defense of the Faith*, and especially Van Til's critique of Clark in his *Introduction to Systematic Theology*, p. 150ff.

must be the fruit of true repentance (Matt. 3:7-10; Acts 26:20), so also works are the fruit of true faith (James 2:14-26; Eph. 2:10). No person is ever justified apart from works — not as the basis or reason for, but as the *necessary* fruit of, justification. We are justified by faith alone, but the kind of faith that justifies is never alone; faith is like an acorn that produces a tree, or like a seed that grows into a melon. If the seed is good, it will produce good fruit.

Both Imply One Another

A second bond between repentance and faith is the necessary logical connection between them. Repentance is the negative side of conversion and faith the positive, so that one cannot look to Christ alone in faith (positive) without looking away from self in repentance (negative).

Or, as John Murray so eloquently stated:

> The interdependence of faith and repentance can be readily seen when we remember that faith is faith in Christ for salvation from sin. But if faith is directed to salvation from sin, there must be hatred of sin and the desire to be saved from it. Such hatred of sin involves repentance which essentially consists in turning from sin unto God.[32]

In repentance the sinner turns *from* himself and his sins, and in faith he turns *to* Christ and His righteousness. It is as if the person is on a path leading to hell and he realizes his plight, which causes him to reverse directions. Now he is walking in the opposite direction toward heaven. In changing directions, he turned *from* hell *to* heaven. It is not possible to change directions 180 degrees in one's life without turning *from* one direction and *to* another, from Satan to God (Acts 26:18), from darkness to light, from self and one's sins to Christ and His righteousness. The turning itself necessarily involves a *from* and a *to* and that simultaneously. In turning to Christ, he turns from himself; in turning to Christ's works of redemption, he turns from his own sinful works; in turning to God's forgiveness, he turns from his own merits, confessing that he cannot achieve forgiveness of sins. Repentance has as

---

[32] John Murray, *Redemption Accomplished and Applied* (Grand Rapids: Wm. B. Eerdmans Pub. Co., 1973), p. 113.

its object our sins, the holiness of God and our need of pardon, while faith's object is Christ, His person and work, and the mercy of God. Repentance, therefore, is a turning from, and faith, a turning to. Since the turning from implies the turning to, sometimes Scripture uses only repentance to address justification, sometimes only faith, and sometimes both, depending on what the biblical author is emphasizing. He may emphasize the negative (turning from) or the positive (turning to) or both. In conversion, therefore, one turns from his sins and himself and turns to Christ and His righteousness.

The anti-lordship advocates say that one turns to Christ without turning from himself and his sins. The logic of this is amazing: the sinner trying to turn to Christ and still maintain love for his sins, trying to serve two masters. The Lord emphatically stated that one cannot serve two masters (Matt. 6:24; Luke 6:13).

If one turns to Christ without turning from his sins, for what purpose does he trust in Christ? It could not be for forgiveness of sins, according to Dillow's understanding, for he does not need to turn from his sins by acknowledging how horrible they are. Many today in the Word of Faith movement embrace Jesus for health and wealth, but this is not repentance and not faith. They embrace Jesus as a sugar daddy, a genie who will grant them wishes. Even if their view of Jesus were orthodox,[33] they could not be justified with their view of the Gospel. The sinner, however, comes to Christ for one express purpose: to have his sins forgiven (Matt. 9:1ff), to obtain righteousness. If the content or knowledge for embracing the Lord is not biblical, then the person does not have saving faith. Sometimes I hear otherwise evangelical Christians say they came to Christ because they had no meaning in their lives, because they were lonely, or because they had messed up their lives. Though it is true that the loving Jesus cures such problems, these are irrelevant to the Gospel. Because repentance is not preached, many in our churches

---

[33]They deny His deity, say He went to suffer under Satan's tortures in hell, became a sinner, and consequently at His resurrection was the first person to be born again and justified. I have written a large work on the movement, entitled *Man as God: The Word of Faith Movement*, which may be ordered from the publisher at the front of this book.

"believe" in Jesus for the fringe benefits, rejecting the essence, and Dillow and Hodges, who do not preach repentance and say "God loves you and has a wonderful plan for your life," are encouraging this.[34] Faith reaches out to the only object for our pardon —Jesus, and repentance gives the only reason for trusting in Him — we are sinners in need of forgiveness. These two aspects are inseparable. Dillow and Hodges promote a sinner coming to Christ for forgiveness of sins while still loving his sins, asking Christ to forgive him but also to allow him to continue practicing sin.

What would you think if a man raped your daughter and said to you: "Please forgive me, but I intend to do it again"? Would it not be obvious that he was not really sorry for his sin and that his request for forgiveness was a farce? He would be asking for forgiveness while not turning and acknowledging his sins as wrong and despicable, not dealing with the very thing that is the problem. You would rightly be incensed. Similarly, a sinner coming to Christ in this manner would not be turning from his sins, acknowledging what he did was despicable, and thus the reason for coming to Jesus would not be a biblical reason. The Lord sovereignly declared that it is the sick who need the physician, not those who think they are well or who do not want to be well. In this instance, the sinner would be asking to be forgiven the penalty for his sins but to be granted a license to embrace the pollution of his sins. Such a dichotomy in coming to Christ is blasphemous casuistry beyond imagination, and there is a biblical example against this:

> But when he [John the Baptist] saw many of the Pharisees and Sadducees coming to his baptism, he said to them, "Brood of vipers! Who has warned you to flee from the wrath to come? Therefore bear fruits worthy of repentance, and do not think to say to yourselves, 'We have Abraham as our father.' For I say to you that God is able to raise up children to Abraham from these stones" (Matt. 3:7-9).

John the Baptist rightly turned away those who tried to trust

---

[34]God indeed has a "wonderful" plan for everyone's life: that the reprobate go to hell and glorify His justice, and that the elect go to heaven and glorify both His justice and His grace.

Christ as Savior while rejecting Him as Lord by not acknowledging their sins. Notice also that John stated that repentance
bears fruit, not that the fruit is the repentance. Their profession of "faith" was illegitimate, for the very reason for coming
to Christ is given with one hand but taken back with the other.
This is why conversion is both negative and positive, for the
express purpose one comes *to* Christ necessarily involves
turning *from* one's sins. And the turning is not obedience as
a pre-condition to faith but confessing that he is a sinner, that
he cannot justify himself, that he is sick and needs the Great
Physician, the obedience being the necessary fruit, as John
the Baptist demanded.

Though repentance and faith are inseparable, we might
ask which comes first logically. Many reformed argue that
faith produces repentance.[35] However, R. L. Dabney, who
argues that they imply one another, rightly says: "Godly
sorrow for sin must be presupposed or implied in the first
actings of faith, because faith embraces Christ as Savior from
sin."[36] He further says:

> Repentance feels the disease, faith embraces the remedy. But
> when we inquire for the first conscious acting of faith or
> repentance after the instant of the new birth, the result is
> decided by the object to which the soul happens to be first
> directed. If the object of its first regenerate look be its own
> ungodliness, the first conscious exercise will be one of repen-
> tance; but just so surely as the volition is, potentially, in the
> preponderating motive, so surely does that soul look from its
> ungodliness to Christ, the remedy of it; it may be uncon-
> sciously at first, but in due time, consciously.[37]

Thus in conversion one cannot look to Christ for pardon
without recognizing his need of pardon, and conversely one
cannot recognize his need of forgiveness — under true con-
viction of sin and regeneration — without looking to Christ.
They imply one another. In turning from one's sins to Christ,
the sinner is implicitly embracing Jesus as Lord. No one is
telling the sinner *to obey* God's commands as a condition for

---

[35]For instance, see William G. T. Shedd in *Dogmatic Theology*, 2:536.

[36]R. L. Dabney, *Lectures in Systematic Theology*, p. 657.

[37]Ibid., p. 658.

justification, but *to recognize* his sinfulness because he has violated God's law. In hating his sins, he has embraced Jesus as Lord, and he has turned from darkness to light, from Satan to God, from himself to Christ, from his sins to God's Word. The fruit of this conversion is obedience and holiness, "without which no one shall see the Lord" (Heb. 12:14).

Hodges and Dillow have never understood this. They think that the Reformed present repentance as works, rather than works as the fruit of repentance. They think that the Reformed say that repentance *is* works, with the works being a condition for justification rather than the necessary evidence. They think the Reformed concept of conversion is works in repentance plus faith plus commitment rather than a turning from sin to Jesus with a faith that commits. Consequently, to keep works out of justification they have gone to the extreme of eliminating works altogether, making them totally optional even as a fruit, thinking that if we make works necessary at any point that we have fallen into legalism. They have, however, fallen headlong into license.[38]

All believers, therefore, have turned from sin (and are

---

[38]The reader may wish to read R. L. Dabney in *Discussions*, vol. 1, pp. 169-228, written 100 years ago to see that the Plymouth Brethren, who were the dispensationalists then, had the same incorrect view of faith and repentance. These errant views have been in their system from the beginning, and they have never taken the time to understand the Reformed or the Bible in these matters. They are long on eschatology and short on the "weightier matters of the law," having a tendency to parrot one another's caricatures. It was heart-breaking while a student at DTS to see these men so unwilling to interact with the Reformed writings. I asked one professor if he had read the Westminster Confession of Faith, to which he said, "No, I would disagree with its eschatology." A professor with a doctor's degree who had never read the main protestant document of all time is not what I would call an educated man. Another professor stated that even the great Dr. John Owen in his volume ten on "limited" atonement could not answer 2 Peter 2:1 as he had not dealt with it anywhere in the tome. Right after class I went to the library and looked it up in the index, and there it was with a very good explanation. I xeroxed it, gave it to the professor, who hesitatingly admitted that he had not read the work! Dabney states of the Plymouth Brethren of his day: "But we especially desire to caution the reader against their tendencies in the following directions: Their wresting of the doctrine of faith and assurance, and entire depreciation of all subjective marks of a state of grace; their denial of the imputation of Christ's active obedience; their disavowal . . . of progressive sanctification, confusion of justification and sanctification, and assertion of a dual nature in the regenerate, suggesting . . . the worst results of antinomianism. . . ." (p. 171).

doing so) and are trusting in and resting on Christ alone for acceptance with God. To rest in Him alone necessarily entails turning from our works or self-reliance.

Both Embrace Jesus as Lord

Those who say Christ can be Savior without being Lord not only destroy the nature of saving faith and repentance, but they also misunderstand the word "Lord" as used with Jesus. Charles Ryrie wants "Lord" as applied to Jesus in the New Testament to mean God but not master. He denies that "Lord" in Romans 10:9-10 means anything more than God.[39] He quotes several commentators who rightly point out that "Lord" means God (v. 13 is a quote of Joel 2:32 where "Lord" is Yhwh and applied to Jesus), but most of these commentators would not deny that "Lord" also implies master. Indeed, Ryrie commits a logical error by thinking that because "Lord" means God that the idea of "master" is thereby eliminated. But how Jesus could be God without being master is an indomitable mystery, for the very nature of God is a sovereign being who does what He pleases and commands His subjects what He desires. What is the New Testament idea of Jesus as Lord?

First, the Greek lexicons — both Arndt and Gingrich and Thayer — give a major meaning of "Lord" as master as well as God. In fact, John 20:28 makes a distinction between Lord and God: "Thomas answered and said to Him, 'My Lord and my God!'"

Secondly, God's Word is clear that "Lord" connotes — if not denotes — obedience. In John 13:37 He is the Lord who gives an example for the disciples to obey. And in Luke 6:46 Jesus says, "Why do you call Me, 'Lord, Lord,' and do not do what I say?" Luke 19:27 is even stronger, "These enemies of mine, who do not want Me to reign over them, bring them here, and slay them in My presence." If one does not want Christ as Lord, he is killed and goes to hell.

The Lord said that if one refused to confess Him before men that He would refuse to confess him before His Father, which would mean one's eternal ruin: "Therefore whoever confesses Me before men, him I will also confess before My

---

[39]Ryrie, *So Great Salvation*, p. 71.

Father who is in heaven. But whoever denies Me before men, him I will also deny before My Father who is in heaven" (Matt. 10:32, 33).

Read these passages and see that by virtue of His resurrection, He is invested with universal dominion as Lord:

> Then Jesus came and spoke to them, saying, "All authority has been given to Me in heaven and on earth" (Matt. 28:18).

> . . . which He worked in Christ when He raised Him from the dead and seated Him at His right hand in the heavenly places, far above all principality and power and might and dominion, and every name that is named, not only in this age but also in that which is to come. And He put all things under His feet, and gave Him to be head over all things to the church, which is His body, the fullness of Him who fills all in all (Eph. 1:20-23).

> Therefore let all the house of Israel know assuredly that God has made this Jesus, whom you crucified, both Lord and Christ (Acts 2:36).

> The word which [God] sent to the children of Israel, preaching peace through Jesus Christ — *He is Lord of all* — that word you know, which was proclaimed throughout all Judea, and began from Galilee after the baptism which John preached: how God anointed Jesus of Nazareth with the Holy Spirit and with power, who went about doing good and healing all who were oppressed by the devil, for God was with Him (Acts 10:36-38).

> There is also an antitype which now saves us, namely baptism (not the removal of the filth of the flesh, but the answer of a good conscience toward God), through the resurrection of Jesus Christ, who has gone into heaven and is at the right hand of God, angels and authorities and powers having been made subject to Him (1 Peter 3:21-22).

Of course some wiseacre will object that the word "Lord" is not used in all the passages I cited, but the idea is certainly there. One may object that though "Lord" may mean master the believer does not need to adhere to this for justification, but this is to divide what God has joined, to use the disparity hermeneutic to make casuistic distinctions where none exist, and where the New Testament gives no hint that such was in the writers' minds. Ryrie would have the new believer understand the same word "Lord" as God but not as master, an oxymoron of the highest order.

According to Romans 10:9-10, confession or belief involves two things: that Jesus is Lord[40] and that He has been bodily[41] resurrected from the dead. One implies the other, but Paul makes them both explicit.

The history of the expression "Jesus is Lord" is also very enlightening.[42] The Roman emperors Augustus (31 B.C.-A.D. 14) and Tiberius (A.D. 14-37) rejected the expression "Lord." But Caligula (A.D. 37-41) accepted it. From Nero (A.D. 54-68) on, who is described in an inscription as "Lord of all the world," the title Lord is very common both of him and of many Roman emperors. Paul was contemporary with Nero! In fact the same Greek construction, Lord Nero or Nero is Lord, is used many times in the papyri and ostraca of Nero. "It was against such a religious claim, which demanded so much of the burdened conscience, that the Christians turned and rejected the totalitarian attitudes of the state."[43] The Roman emperors did not mind its citizens worshipping any god they chose as long as once a year they proclaimed the Caesar as the ultimate Lord, meaning that Caesar was the Lord of lords. And the emperors did not think of the divine title Lord without the implication of obedience, for if this had been so, why did they murder so many Christians for refusing to obey them? The Caesar claimed ultimate lordship and thus

---

[40]That "Jesus is Lord" is the correct translation, see 1 Corinthians 12:3 [κυριον Ιησουν]; Philippians 2:11 [κυριος Ιησους χριστος]; 1 Corinthians 8:5-6. See A. T. Robertson, *Word Pictures in the New Testament* (Nashville: Broadman Press, 1931), 4:389; and his grammar on the double accusative, *A Grammar of the Greek New Testament in the Light of Historical Research*, p. 1123.

[41]Some, like the Jehovah's Witnesses, deny His bodily resurrection, maintaining that He was raised a spirit creature.

[42]The history is from: Adolph Deismann, *Light from the Ancient East* (Grand Rapids: Baker Book House, 1978), pp. 350-357; Colin Brown, *The New International Dictionary of New Testament Theology* (Grand Rapids: Zondervan, 1971), 2:511-515; C. E. B. Cranfield, *The International Critical Commentary: The Epistle to the Romans* (Edinburgh: T. & T. Clark, 1979), 2:526ff.

[43]*New International Dictionary of the NT Theology*, vol. 2:511.

the right of absolute obedience, which directly conflicted with
Jesus.[44] The expression that Jesus is Lord, therefore, was both
religious and political, and precisely meant that *He* was God
and master — not the Roman emperors! As Deismann so
beautifully expressed:

> . . . the Christian exclusive confession of "our Lord Jesus
> Christ," which could not but sound dangerous to a Roman
> official (since from Domitian onwards the title "our lord" was
> applied to the Caesars), led to Christian martyrdoms. . . . In
> the case of Polycarp, at Smyrna in the year 155, it was a
> question of the "lord" formula. "What is the harm in saying
> 'lord Caesar'?" the Irenarch Herod and his father Nicetes
> asked the saint seductively. The scene enacted on 17 July 180
> at Carthage before the judgment-seat of the Proconsul P.
> Vigellius Saturninus stands out even more plainly. The Ro-
> man official commands the Christian Speratus of Scili in
> Numidia: "Swear by the genius of our lord Emperor!" And
> the Christian answers: "I know no imperium of this world, . . .
> I know my Lord, the King of kings, and Emperor of all
> nations."[45]

In the Orient "Lord" was a very common term for their
deities and "the kings of the East have from time immemorial
been 'lords,' and their subjects nothing better than slaves." In
Egypt it had been very common to address the Pharoah as "O
king, our lord." Ptolemy XIII was addressed as "the lord king
god," and in the time of Alexander the Great, Ptolemy and
Cleopatra are called "the lords, the most great gods."[46] So
Paul considered himself a slave or "bond servant" of Jesus the
Lord.

The Lordship of Christ was also based on Psalm 110:1
(Matt. 22:44; 26:64; Mark 12:36; 14:62, 16:19; Luke 20:42ff;
22:69; Acts 2:34; 1 Cor. 15:25; Eph. 1:20; Col. 3:1; Heb. 1:3,

---

[44]I cannot resist the application that our own government is making the same
claim today, not caring what god one worships as long as its citizens give
ultimate allegiance and confession to it. Thus Jesus has no place in the public
arena, in government, in our schools, in the officials we elect, in the laws of
sexuality and abortion. "There is nothing new under the sun."

[45]Deismann, p. 356.

[46]All from Deismann.

13; 10:12ff; 12:2), which is the most quoted Old Testament passage in the New Testament. Thus the title that "Jesus is Lord" was originated from the Old Testament but also was very appropriate in the political setting of the early church.

Going back to Romans 10:9, Cranfield rightly articulates:

> . . . the confession that Jesus is Lord meant the acknowledgment that Jesus shares the name and the nature, the holiness, the authority, power, majesty and eternity of the one and only true God. And, when, as is often the case, there is joined with the title kurios [Lord] a personal pronoun in the genitive, there is expressed in addition the sense of His ownership of those who acknowledge Him and of their consciousness of being His property, the sense of personal commitment and allegiance, of trust and confidence.[47]

When Paul and the Spirit of God penned Romans 10:9-10, *they* knew the implication of what they wrote: Nero be hanged, Jesus is Lord and master!

Ryrie would have the Christians confessing two lords, Caesar and Jesus, dividing the one word "Lord" into two distinct concepts, separating sanctification from justification. Again his hermeneutic of distinctions leads to dividing Jesus, but the Lord demands that He alone be one's master. After Christianity became a legal religion, the emperors adopted the title *Despotes* in lieu of the title Lord, recognizing Jesus as the ultimate master, so even they understand that there could only be one master.

What is the Relationship of Faith to Works?

The WCF reflects Scripture in making works the effect of saving faith. Clark objects to the expression that faith *includes* works,[48] preferring to say that faith *produces* good works. Other Reformed seem to have no problem with the word "include." Faith/repentance by its very nature includes the idea of obedience, for in hating one's own sins and in embrac-

---

[47]Cranfield, Op. Cit., p. 529.

[48]Clark, *Faith and Saving Faith*, p. 92.

ing Christ as the cure, he has implicitly endeavored to walk in His commands (WCF: 15.2). The commands reveal our sins, so in *turning* from our sins, that is, in *acknowledging* them as heinous in God's eyes, we implicitly love His commands. There is no neutrality. Through faith alone the sinner embraces Jesus as His Lord and Savior, and in the reflex action of faith he engages in good works.

Faith versus Works

Dillow believes that genuine faith can exist apart from works and by implication that one can have evangelical obedience apart from faith. For example, he says: "The land will be obtained only on the condition of faith plus obedience" (p. 50). Again he says, "While Abraham received justification by faith alone, it is clear that he could only obtain the inheritance by means of obedience" (p. 54). Commenting on James 2 where God says that faith without works is dead (vv. 17, 20), Dillow says: "They will be saved in the sense of finding deliverance from the spiritually impoverishing consequences of sin, not by faith alone, but by faith plus their works of obedience" (p. 190). According to Dillow, we have faith, then later obedience, which places obedience outside of faith, or at least allows faith to exist without obedience. By "faith alone" Dillow means a faith devoid of works so that if works come later, they are an addition to faith. Abraham allegedly received one blessing by faith and another by obedience.

Faith and Merit

There are several blatant errors that Dillow commits. First, there is the grave theological error of synergism, the teaching that it takes both God and man to save man. The first part of salvation is by faith and the second part by works, or having begun in the Spirit we are now perfected by the flesh, contrary to Galatians 3:3 (see below). At another place, Dillow states: "Not only had she given her life to Christ, but she had also *allowed* Christ to be formed in her" (p. 61) [emphasis added]. What "giving one's life to Christ" has to do with the Gospel, Dillow does not state[49] (which sounds like lordship salvation),

---

[49]Evangelicalism abounds with many inaccurate statements regarding the Gospel: "Give your life to Christ"; "Ask Jesus into your heart"; "Give your

but the second part definitely demonstrates that man is the boss in salvation. Synergism has been repeatedly condemned in the church for centuries, being a denial of the Gospel.

How is this a denial of the Gospel? As we have seen, faith cannot exist without works. We do not have two separate entities co-existing independently: faith and then optionally works. Though faith is not obedience, faith itself produces obedience. Dillow, however, has a faith that produces no works and then later, at the option of the "saved" saint, he may produce works in addition to faith. The former is justification without the effect of works, and the latter is sanctification by works. In neither case do we have biblical truth. A justification void of works is the heresy of license, and sanctification by human works is the heresy of legalism. What Scripture presents is a living faith that embraces Jesus for justification and sanctification, which in turn necessarily produces works. The Puritans used the example of the eye, which is the only instrument of the body that sees, but it never exists independent of the body.

Good works in the life of a Christian do not exist independent of faith, as Dillow implies, but all good works are produced by faith. In fact, our faith is imperfect in this life, as Dillow admits, and yet he has us producing works that are so good that they merit God's working, making Him our debtor. There is no work of a Christian that is perfect, but they are accepted by God on the basis of the substitutionary death of Jesus. For a work to be perfect, the person would have to be sinless, have perfect faith, obey every portion of the law outwardly and especially inwardly. Inwardly, he must have motives for the glory of God alone and do the work solely for Him and for others. No one this side of heaven can do this. Dillow tries to qualify himself by saying that faith can

---

heart to Jesus"; "Invite Christ into your life," etc. These are not rank heresies but do not address the point at issue in the Gospel, which is that man is a sinner needing righteousness. We trust in Jesus for forgiveness of our sins, for righteousness, for eternal life (Acts 2:38; 13:38, 39; Rom. 4:1-10; 10:9, 10; Gal. 2:16, etc). The Lord automatically comes into our hearts when we believe in Him so why would we want to make this a condition for the Gospel when this is an effect of the Gospel? Likewise, we do not say, "Have you asked Jesus to seal you with His Spirit?" because He automatically does this when we believe (Eph. 1:13, 14).

later produce our works. But if so, then Dillow has himself on the horns of a dilemma: either faith has a volitional aspect to produce the works (contrary to his belief) or works exist independent of faith.

No Christian can make God his debtor by what he does as Dillow wrongly assumes. Since our best works reveal that we have only done our duty as unprofitable servants (Luke 17:10), we can merit nothing. The rewards we receive are given to us for Jesus' sake, and the very works we do are produced in us by the Holy Spirit. Where is the merit in this? Dillow rightly rages against our works as meriting nothing in justification, but then he has our works meriting everything in sanctification, even meriting sanctification itself. According to Dillow, the Cross of Jesus merited us grace for justification, but it is up to the saint to merit sanctification apart from the Cross. Jesus did His part, and allegedly we must do ours, completing the salvation that He began. With Dillow's doctrine, He who began a good work in us will perform it until the day of Jesus Christ (Phil. 1:6) — if we let Him, if we merit it. Dillow's reading of the verse would be that He who began a good work in us will be supplemented, confirmed, and completed by us — maybe.

Furthermore, if our works merit sanctification, there is a second and optional work of grace after conversion. In this idea, the Gospel is necessary but not sufficient, necessary to keep one out of hell but not sufficient to save one completely. The Gospel of justification is the first step toward salvation, taken by grace alone, but the rest is up to the saint (more on this shortly).

This further means, of course, that the Spirit's "hands" are tied, that He cannot sanctify us without our permission. This in turn leads to the conclusion that our sins hinder His working in conforming us to Christ, which logically implies that the Cross did not deal with the power of sin in our lives but only the penalty of sin. But if the Cross did remove all obstacles to our full salvation (justification, sanctification, and glorification), then what hinders our sanctification?

If the Cross dealt with sin's penalty but not its power, we have divided sin into two classes, which Scripture knows nothing about (more interpretive distinctions!). When Adam sinned, he legally came under the judgment of God and morally was polluted, both from the one sin (Rom. 5:12ff). When man is conceived, he legally comes under Adam's sin and is morally polluted. When one comes to Christ, he is legally acquitted and morally cleansed. In each case, the moral aspect (impartation) is a necessary effect of the legal (imputation). Since sin cannot be divided, neither can its reversal — salvation.

By contrast, the Spirit has no hindrance in sanctifying us, for Jesus paid it all. But if the Holy Spirit cannot sanctify us because of our sin, then what was the Cross for? If some sin — such as refusing His lordship — hinders the Spirit's working, then there must be some sin Jesus did not die for. If there is some sin Jesus did not die for that we can remove by our works, why do we need Him at all? In this scheme, one enters the Christian life by way of the Cross but continues the Christian life without the Cross, or at least the Cross is secondary to our works, contrary to Galatians 3:3 (see below). If Jesus died for all the sins of His elect — and He did — then all hindrance to removing the pollution of these sins in our lives has been removed. Grace, then, is irresistible, or simply a free gift.

Someone may object that Jesus did die for all our sins and that the only hindrance is our volition. All we must do is "appropriate" the grace. Our response is where do we get the grace to use our wills in "appropriating" grace? If from ourselves, then why do we need Jesus? Why can't we do it all? If we can do some things right, what hinders us from doing all things right? (We have an incipient perfectionism.) If we must let Him sanctify us, where do we get the grace to do this? This is nothing more than a salvation by the will of man,[50] which Scripture specifically denies many times (John 1:13; Rom. 9:16; John 6:44, 45; Matt. 11:25-27; etc). As Warfield so accurately stated: "If this be true, then it is not Christ who regulates our activities, and so secures our sanctification; but we who regulate His activities, and so secure our own sanctification."[51] Again he says, "It is our faith which regulates our

---

[50]*Autosoterism* is the accurate term Warfield uses in *The Plan of Salvation.*

[51]Warfield, *Perfectionism*, p. 246.

grace; and that means that it is we and not God who saves."[52]

Consider though that just as the saint produces good works by his faith in Christ, the ungodly produce the works of the flesh from unbelief. If the saint can have good works apart from the volition in faith as Dillow implies, then by analogy the sinner can have bad works apart from the volition in unbelief. The mother of all good works or bad works is faith or unbelief. Can you conceive of a person who does not believe in Jesus not producing the works of the flesh? Conversely, can you conceive of a believer in Jesus who has the Holy Spirit not producing the fruit of the Spirit?

Faith and James 2

A second series of errors Dillow commits are severe exegetical errors in James 2. Like Zane Hodges, he thinks that one can have dead faith and still be a Christian. Dillow says that if the faith is dead, it must have been alive once (p. 188ff). This is a false inference, for James' point is that a non-working faith is lifeless and a living faith produces works. The word "dead" in Greek and in English does not necessarily imply previous life, and the Arndt and Gingrich Greek lexicon gives "useless" as the meaning of dead in James 2:26. James illustrates his point using the word "dead" not only of a dead body but also of helping a brother and of demons who "believe." Was the "dead" faith of the brother who was derelict regarding his duty once alive, or were the demons also once alive? The Christian brother and the demons had *useless* faith. Also we can see what "dead" means by contrasting it with its opposite: Abraham and Rahab were "justified by works" or by a living faith. The kind of faith that justified them was living, vibrant, demonstrating itself in their lives.

Dillow thinks that the salvation of which James speaks is of the physical life and of sanctification. James says it is justification: "Was not Abraham our father justified by works when he offered Isaac his son on the altar?" (v. 21). "You see then that a man is justified by works, and not by faith only" (v. 24). James quotes the same verse as Paul in Romans 4:3 to prove justification by faith alone: "And the Scripture was fulfilled which says, 'Abraham believed God, and it was

---

[52]Ibid., p. 273.

accounted to him for righteousness. And he was called the friend of God'" (v. 23). James is saying by metonymy of effect (putting the effect for the cause) that Abraham was justified by "works," that is, a working faith, and that "faith alone" or faith by itself without works (read an empty profession) is useless and the person not justified. Dillow says that true faith can exist alone while James says it cannot. Dillow says James is speaking of sanctification, but James says justification.

Dillow emphatically says that faith is never qualified in the New Testament: "Nowhere in the New Testament are adverbs, such as 'truly' or 'really' believed, ever used" (p. 325). Perhaps the word "adverb" is too limited, and of course he denies this passage in James. There are, however, such qualifications:

> Now the purpose of the commandment is love from a pure heart, from a good conscience, and from *sincere faith* (1 Tim. 1:5).

> I call to remembrance the *genuine faith* that is in you, which dwelt first in your grandmother Lois and your mother Eunice, and I am persuaded is in you also (2 Tim. 1:5).

> They profess to know God, but in works they deny Him, being abominable, disobedient, and disqualified for every good work (Titus 1:16).

> Now by this we know that we know Him, if we keep His commandments. He who says, "I know Him," and does not keep His commandments, is a liar, and the truth is not in him (1 John 2:3-4).

Finally, Dillow promotes a faith that is purely a passive mental act, not active. By passive he means "the will plays no part" (p. 276). He is confident that "Neither Alexander or Warfield nor a host of other Reformed theologians, including Calvin himself, ever taught that faith included obedience" (p. 283).[53] If by "included" Dillow means that faith is the works,

---

[53]Dillow probably got this from Clark, *Faith and Saving Faith*, p. 92. If so, Dillow has typically either misunderstood Clark or misrepresented him, for Clark states on the same page that no Calvinist theologian ever stated that Christ could be your Savior without being your Lord. When Clark says that assent does not *include* good works, he quickly adds that good works necessarily follow assent.

then we agree. Further in his discussion, however, it becomes obvious that he means that faith cannot innately lead to works. It can if it wants to but not necessarily. Regarding such incredible ignorance, it is obvious that he has not read the Reformed theologians, and we offer the following Reformed quotes:

> [James] says that faith is dead, being by itself, that is, when destitute of good works. . . . Then he [James] bids to show faith without works, and thus reasons from what is impossible, to prove what does not exist. . . . The meaning then is, "Unless thy faith brings forth fruits, I deny that thou hast any faith." . . . James . . . shows that good works are always connected with faith.[54]

> By this faith a Christian . . . yields obedience to the commands. . . . These good works, done in obedience to God's commandments, are the fruits and evidences of a true and lively faith (WCF: 14.2; 16.2).

> That faith which secures eternal life . . . works by love, and is fruitful in good works. . . .[55]

> The faith which justifies is no dead faith, but a faith which works by love. It admires the beauty of holiness as well as the glory of the Savior, and contains in it the very seeds of repentance. It never embraces Christ without renouncing sin. . . .[56]

> There is a volitional aspect of faith, in which it appears to the man who believes to be induced by a conscious effort of his will, a conscious effort of his will by which he resolves to cease trying to save himself and resolves to accept the salvation offered by Christ.[57]

> The faith that Paul means when he speaks of justification by

---

[54] John Calvin, Commentary on James 2:14ff.

[55] Charles Hodge, *Systematic Theology* (Grand Rapids: Wm. B. Eerdmans Pub. Co, 1968), 3:68.

[56] James Henly Thornwell, *The Collected Writings of James Henley Thornwell* (Edinburgh: Banner of Truth Trust, 1986), 2:30-40.

[57] J. Gresham Machen, *What Is Faith?* (Grand Rapids: Wm. B. Eerdmans Pub. Co, 1965), p. 197.

faith alone is a faith that works.[58]

. . . faith is a volitional as well as an intellectual activity. . . .[59]

. . . a true faith produces good works. There is an agricultural expression which puts the matter succinctly enough: faith is the root and works are the fruit. We cannot be saved without them.[60]

At the same time good works necessarily follow from the union of believers with Christ . . . and as the fruits of faith.[61]

Faith is passive in receiving the free gift of forgiveness of sins but active in its expression in living for God. According to Berkhof, "While the Roman Catholics stressed the fact that justifying faith is merely assent and has its seat in the understanding, the Reformers regarded it as trust, having its seat in the will."[62] Dillow's concept is Roman Catholic.

Conclusion

Those who deny biblical repentance, likewise deny that Christ must be Lord as well as Savior; they affirm the nature of faith as understanding only, and teach that one is justified by simple profession or repetition of words. These concepts stand or fall together. Truly we are living in a man-centered age that despises holiness unto God, making it optional at every turn. Yet the truth is that conversion is a unified whole, being composed of turning from one's sins to Christ and bowing to Him as Lord, with the evidence being discernible in one's life. As God says, "Let everyone who names the name of the Lord abstain from wickedness" (2 Tim. 2:19).

Consider what a monstrosity Dillow promotes. From a

---

[58]Ibid., p. 204.

[59]Gordon Clark, *Faith and Saving Faith* (Jefferson, MD: The Trinity Foundation, 1983), p. 65.

[60]Gordon Clark, *What Do Presbyterians Believe?* (Phillipsburg, NJ: Presbyterian and Reformed Pub. Co., 1979), p. 163. If true faith blooms into good works, the works are in some way contained in or included in saving faith.

[61]L. Berkhof, *Systematic Theology*, p. 543.

[62]Ibid., p. 496-97.

chopped-up hermeneutic, he has a chopped-up Christ, a chopped-up faith, and a chopped-up salvation. Only the mind of man "believes" in Jesus, and this "faith" does not include works. What kind of salvation excludes the kingship of Jesus in the word "Lord," excludes sanctification from justification, and excludes the will from faith? Only part of man (mind) embraces part of Christ (priesthood) who in turn only saves part of man (from hell but optionally from himself and his personal sins). What kind of salvation gives the sinner legal righteousness that keeps him out of hell but only makes moral righteousness possible, allowing him to wallow in the power of sin the rest of his life? What kind of regeneration renews man's mind but leaves his will "free" to choose sin and Satan or Jesus as equally optional masters?

One other point. Suppose the saint dies and does not want to be glorified. Suppose he likes his sins and wants to be in heaven with them. God allegedly cannot overcome his will, so what will happen then if the saint does not give God permission to glorify him? If the person says that God does so anyway, then why cannot God sanctify him now without his permission? Indeed, why is it that regeneration has not changed the person so that now he wants sanctification and glorification? Suppose the saint has been so wicked that God had to kill him to take him home (as Dillow alleges). Does not this mean that God's grace is irresistible, that God will not allow His child to wallow in sin? If God can "force" His will on him at death, why not now? What is different about the point of death from the rest of his life? What would you think of a parent who only did what was right for his children when they let him? You would rightly think he was a sorry parent. God is a good parent, even "whipping" us out of love when we need it (Heb. 12:5-14); His sanctifying grace is irresistible and free like justifying grace.

4

Justification and Sanctification

Now we shall consider justification and sanctification, and especially the relationship between the two with the implications regarding perseverance and easy believism. If sanctification necessarily follows justification and is not based on one's works, then perseverance is established.

What Is the Relationship of Justification to Sanctification?

The relationship between justification and sanctification is cause to effect. Justification is rightly termed the legal act of God and sanctification the moral flower that blooms from it. Just as the imputation of Adam's sin carries with it the impartation of corruption of heart and nature, so also the imputation of Christ's righteousness brings the impartation of holiness in the believer's life. Let us look at this relationship between the two.

Virtually no orthodox person would doubt that justification is a legal act by God. By legal we mean that God declares the sinner right with Him even though the person is still a sinner. The sinner has been forgiven of his sins and given the righteousness of Christ. From Romans 4 this is obvious, for in verses 1-10 Paul teaches in no uncertain terms that a person's sins are forgiven and the righteousness of Christ given to him even while he is still a sinner. The terms used are legal courtroom terms: justified, forgiven, reckoned, imputed, sin not taken into account, and so on. This is the heart of the Gospel, that a sinner who deserves hell is given right standing with God even though his character is still stained with sin.

Of course such a doctrine has caused the less than orthodox to say that Protestants teach a license to sin, for if one is declared to be right with God even while he is still a sinner, how he lives must not matter. Paul realized that his teaching led to this objection, for in Romans 6:1 he anticipated: "What shall we say then? Are we to continue in sin that grace may increase?" His answer was succinct: "May it never be!" (v. 2). Dillow would have Paul say: "You shouldn't continue in sin, but you can if you insist."

Legal versus Moral (can be distinguished)

Paul also maintains that the one who is justified also is sanctified. In other words, once the sinner is declared righteous, then God begins to make him righteous by sanctification, by making him like the Lord Jesus in his moral character. One either has both justification and sanctification or neither. Sanctification follows inevitably on the heels of justification.[1] The following contrast between them may be helpful, but just keep in mind that because they can be distinguished does not mean they are two separate graces. The reader is encouraged to look up the references to see that the comments are true and to see that sanctification is designed by God to follow justification.

(1) Justification is a *legal act* by which the righteous Judge acquits the sinner and accepts him as righteous, though I am still sinful (Rom. 4:1-13; 8:32-34). If justification were a moral act, as the Roman Catholic Church maintains to this day, then we would be in bondage to works, for God would not accept us until we had reached a state of moral perfection. The reason they maintain that works are necessary for salvation is that they make the moral work of sanctification a condition for justification. Sanctification, however, is an *ethical process*

---

[1] Charles Hodge in *The Life of Faith* says that faith especially embraces Christ for justification and repentance turns from one's sins for sanctification. Though this may lead some to make a wall between faith and repentance, there is an element of truth in Hodge's statement. Of course, faith embraces Christ for sanctification, too, as the Westminster Confession states.

by which the Holy Spirit makes the saint righteous, conforming him to Christ (Phil. 3:21; Col. 3:10; Rom. 6:1-14; 8:1-16).

(2) Justification is *objective*: a declaration that the sinner is righteous, which does not affect the sinner's personal pollution within (Gal. 2:16). He is outwardly clothed with Christ's righteousness. Sanctification is *subjective*: The Spirit works within the saint to produce faith and Christ-like-ness (Phil. 2:12, 13). Inwardly he is being made like Jesus (1 John 3:3).

(3) Justification is *substitutionary*: based on the death of Christ in the sinner's place (1 Peter 2:24; Mark 10:45). Sanctification is *not substitutionary:* The Spirit irresistibly enables the saint himself to do good works (Phil. 2:12, 13; 1 John 3:9; 5:18).

(4) Justification is the *ground for sanctification*, for God cannot conform one to Christ until the sin question of that sinner has been settled (Rom. 5:21-6:2). Sanctification is *justification in action*, for God will surely continue what He has begun (Phil. 1:6).

(5) Justification is *not a process* but a once for all completed act of God (Rom. 5:1). Sanctification is a *process* that is not completed in this life (1 John 1:6-10; 3:2, 3).

(6) Justification is God's work *for us* in Christ two thousand years ago (Rom. 5:8). Sanctification is God's work *in us* now by the Holy Spirit (2 Thess. 2:13).

(7) Justification delivers *once for all from the penalty of the sin* of transgressing God's law (Rom. 6:23; 1 John 3:4). In sanctification the saint *is being continually saved from the power* of indwelling sin (Eph. 4:20-24; 1 John 3:9; Rom. 8:1-11).

(8) Justification is *imputed righteousness,* which is like a coat worn on the outside. Sanctification is *imparted righteousness,* which is being made holy on the inside.

(9) In justification imputed righteousness gives the sinner eternal and irrevocable *standing with God*. In sanctification imparted righteousness *displays to man* that the saint is God's, without which no saint shall see the Lord (Heb. 12:14).

Legal then Moral (cause/effect)

There is, of course, an inherent and inseparable connection between the two. Justification *always comes first logically*[2] *and*

---

[2]We say logically because there is no time delay between the two. Sanctification

is always followed by sanctification automatically. Dillow uses the word "automatic," and as Pete Frye has pointed out, the word says too little and too much. It says too little, implying that God is not involved in sanctification but that some natural force takes over and proceeds involuntarily. It says too much, suggesting that God and His grace are subject to cause and effect. But we use the word in rebuttal to Dillow, understanding that sanctification is "automatic" because "He who has begun a good work in you will complete it until the day of Jesus Christ" (Phil. 1:6). God is at work in the believer. As Paul said in Colossians 2:6: "As you have therefore received Christ Jesus the Lord, so walk in Him." Thus he expected the "walking" (sanctification) to follow the "receiving" (justification). Furthermore, as the WCF makes abundantly clear, the believer is not justified for works done before or after justification:

> Those whom God effectually calleth he also freely justifieth; *not by infusing righteousness into them,* but by pardoning their sins, and by accounting and accepting their persons as righteous: *not for any thing wrong in them, or done by them,* but for Christ's alone: *not by imputing faith itself, the act of believing, or any other evangelical obedience, to them as their righteousness*; but by imputing the obedience and satisfaction of Christ unto them, they receiving and resting on him and his righteousness by faith: which faith they have not of themselves; it is the gift of God (WCF: 11.1).

But the Confession also rightly states of saints, "Their ability to do good works is not at all of themselves, but wholly from the Spirit of Christ" (WCF: 16.3), and these good works "are the fruits and evidences of a true and lively faith" (WCF: 16.1). Regeneration gives rise to faith, and faith is the sole instrument for justification/sanctification, which in turn produces good works.

In Galatians 3:3 Paul proclaims: "Are you so foolish? Having begun in the Spirit, are you now being made perfect by the flesh?" This verse is antithetical to Dillow and the whole system he and Hodges espouse, for in their view justification occurs first, and then sanctification, if it happens at all, is a

is the immediate effect of justification.

product of the saint's obedience. In other words, Dillow would say that "we began in the Spirit and are made perfect by the flesh," by our obedience, by our submission to some command, by our "appropriation" or use of grace. Justification is a gift by the Spirit, but sanctification is earned by our flesh. Whether we are made perfect or not is up to our flesh, our wills. This point cannot be emphasized too much, for Paul had just stated: "I do not set aside the grace of God; for if righteousness comes through the law [through what I do], then Christ died in vain" (Gal. 2:21).

Of course, Dillow would say that justifying righteousness and sanctifying righteousness are not received the same way, the former being a gift and the latter earned. To say this, though, is to misunderstand the very heart of the Gospel, for the assumption is that we must go on to something more, something higher and grander than the Gospel after conversion. The Gospel is not sufficient for sanctification but only for justification. By contrast, Paul said that if "He who did not spare His own Son, but delivered Him up for us all, how shall He not with Him also freely give us all things?" (Rom. 8:32). If God has given us the greatest gift of all, Jesus, will He not give us all lesser blessings? There is nothing greater than Jesus to advance to. The Gospel alone, faith alone in Jesus alone, is the sole reason we receive justification and sanctification. Indeed, union with Christ, effected when we are called into the fellowship of His Son, guarantees both justification and sanctification (Rom. 6:1ff). How can one be in union with Him and not have the lesser graces (sanctification) when he has the greatest grace, as Paul argues in Romans 8?

Indeed, Dillow's making good works optional and making a deeper relationship with Him dependent on us, reveals a fatal theological flaw: The Gospel is not sufficient for life and godliness. He has denied the Reformation, evangelical *dictum* that faith *alone* in God alone is sufficient for the Christian. According to Dillow, faith is necessary but not sufficient, for we must add our works to His to have all the blessings. Thus faith alone is not sufficient. The Gospel is necessary but not sufficient for all of life, for we must have a work subsequent to conversion. Thus the Gospel *alone* is not enough. The grace of God is necessary but not sufficient as we must add our works to merit a "deeper" relationship, to merit sanctification, and to merit an inheritance. Man's works are the basis for God's gracious operations rather than God's grace the basis for man's works. Grace is necessary but not sufficient. Therefore grace *alone* is not enough. Dillow's system has a divided glory as God is praised for His part but man receives the final praise as nothing would have been accomplished without man's work, without man completing what God had begun or only "made possible." Therefore, God's glory *alone* is not enough.[3]

This is the error of the second and optional work of grace that characterizes the Charismatics with their "baptism in the Holy Spirit," the higher life movement, and Keswick theology.[4] What the Charismatics call the "baptism," higher life terms "letting go and letting God," Keswick "yielding to the Spirit," Dillow calls optional sanctification. The terms differ, but the substance is the same: more than the Gospel is needed for the truly advanced Christian life. After conversion comes the truly great part of the Christian life, the "more" that God did not include in the initial offer. And we gain this "more," not by the Holy Spirit, not by the intercession of Jesus, not by our union with Him, but by our works. And Dillow has the audacity to refer to the Reformed view of faith as another Gospel, a Gospel of legalism!

What is implicit in Dillow's theology is that once one takes this advanced and second step of grace, then all is well and easy in the Christian life. This becomes a short-cut to maturity, whereas the biblical way is the slow way through many trials, struggling with sin. Indeed, we must "strengthen the souls of the disciples, exhorting them to continue in the faith, and saying, 'We must through many tribulations *enter* the kingdom of God'" (Acts 14:22). There is no short cut, no instantaneous way to gain this entrance except through perseverance.[5]

---

[3]For an insightful discussion on the sufficiency of grace and faith, see G. C. Berkouwer, *Faith and Sanctification* (Grand Rapids: Wm. B. Eerdmans Pub. Co., 1972), Chapter II: "Sola Fide and Sanctification."

[4]See *Perfectionism* by Warfield. Absolutely must reading regarding these problems of our day.

[5]Though Dillow emphatically maintains that "entering" the kingdom is not the

The reason God justifies us is to make us holy, to sanctify us. Just as justification is a fruit of His Cross so is sanctification, for both have the same goal: conformity to the moral image of Christ. To restate this, glorification is the realization of justification, and sanctification is the practical out-working of justification. Or we could say that once we are justified, God begins in sanctification to make us what He has declared us to be in justification: righteous. He begins this in justification and concludes it in glorification. The whole point of the Gospel is righteousness and that we will be made morally pure like Jesus:

> Who gave Himself for us, that He might *redeem us from every lawless deed and purify for Himself His own special people, zealous for good works* (Titus 2:14).

> . . . just as Christ also loved the church and gave Himself for it, *that He might sanctify and cleanse it with the washing of water by the word, that He might present it to Himself a glorious church, not having spot or wrinkle or any such thing, but that it should be holy and without blemish* (Eph. 5:25-27).

> Just as He chose us in Him before the foundation of the world, *that we should be holy and without blame before Him in love* (Eph. 1:4).

The heart of the Gospel is righteousness: We are sinners under judgment who need perfect righteousness to be accepted by God and to enjoy God. We do not have righteousness; Christ does. When we turn to Him from our sins, God gives us legal standing with Him and then makes us conform to this legal standing by making us holy like Jesus. The Gospel is not possessing eternal life as an abstract concept as if it existed apart from righteousness; the Gospel *is* righteousness. We are legally righteous then morally made holy until we are like Jesus. Why would God legally declare us righteous and then stop His work? This would only be a half Gospel with a

---

same as "inheriting" it (p. 78), Acts 14:22 destroys this distinction. Dillow barely mentions Acts 14:22 (pp. 78, 152). On page 152 he says of Acts 14:22: "It must be possible for them [disciples] not to remain true or there would be no point in taking this trip." Notice once again that he *assumes* that a command to Christians to do something must be optional, and also observe that the text says they *enter* through perseverance, not inherit, which he does not deal with.

half salvation.

In Romans 6:1, Paul asks whether we should continue in sin once we are justified, and he answers his own question with a strong No, stating that those who have died to sin are no longer its slaves (Rom. 6:2). Thus it is clear that once one is justified, Paul expected sanctification to follow automatically.

Some elaboration on this passage is needful. In Romans 6-8 Paul discusses sanctification after his lengthy presentation of justification in chapters 3-5. In Romans 6:1-11 the Apostle proclaims that the one who has been justified has also died to sin's power by identification with Christ in His death and resurrection. Some want to state that this is "positionally" true but not necessarily practically true in the believer's life. They base this on the command in verses 11-13 to present our members and bodies to God. They assume that a command means that the facts Paul stated in verses 1-10 must not be true in the believer's life. Why else, they assert, would Paul give a command if they were already doing it? So Dillow argues (p. 182ff).

In contrast, however, it would be more logical and exegetical to maintain that Paul gives the command to present yourself to God not to make verses 1-10 true but because they are true. In other words, God gives the command to present our bodies to Him only after He has given the grace to obey — not in order to get the grace to obey. In grammatical terms, the "is" (indicative mood) of verses 1-10 becomes the foundation for the "ought" (imperative mood) of verses 11-13. In theological terms, the grace of verses 1-10 is the foundation for the law or obedience of verses 11-13. Thus sanctification inevitably flows from justification.

Naturally Dillow seeks to warp this, stating that the Christian has the option to practice sin, not believing Paul's statement to the contrary (p. 183). Paul gives the reason Christians will obey the commands of 11-13 as seen by the word "for": "*For* sin shall not have dominion over you, for you are not under law but under grace" (Rom. 6:14). There are no if's or but's, just the truth that redeemed man is not under the power of sin any longer, which is to say that sanctification follows justification. Dillow says verse 14 is conditioned by the commands of verses 11-13, but Paul says one does the commands because of the grace God gives in verse 14. Dillow conditions grace on law while Paul conditions law on grace.

In Romans 5-7 there are words used indicating the ruling power of sin and of grace.[6] The words show what is the ruling characteristic of saints and sinners, not giving saints the option to live in sin or degrees between saints. Just a few verses will confirm this:

> Knowing this, that our old man was crucified with [Him], that the body of sin might be done away with, that we should no longer be *slaves* of sin (Rom. 6:6).

> For sin shall not *have dominion* over you, for you are not under law but under grace (Rom. 6:14).

> And having been set free from sin, you became *slaves* of righteousness (Rom. 6:18).

> But now *having been set free* from sin, and having become *slaves* of God, you have your fruit to holiness, and the end, everlasting life (Rom. 6:22).

In each verse notice that the contrast is absolute, between Christians and non-Christians, between the Romans pre-converted and post-converted states.[7] Christians have "once for all died to sin" with Christ (Rom. 6:10).[8] Being in union[9] with

---

[6] The words are *basileuo* (5:14, 17, 21; 6:12), *douleuo* (6:6, 18, 22), *kurieuo* (6:9, 14; 7:1), *doulos* (6:16, 17-20), *eleutheroo* (6:18, 22).

[7] There is absolute depravity, total depravity, and depravity. Those in hell are *absolutely depraved*, as wicked as possible, having not even common grace to retard their wickedness. They vent the full expression of their wickedness. *Total depravity* refers to the condition of the lost on earth who have sin in every part of their beings, being under its dominion, unable to please God, though they do not express their wickedness to its fullest. *Depravity* is the condition of Christians who have sin in every part of their beings but are not under its power any more, being enabled by regeneration and the Spirit to please God, though nothing they do is completely free from sin, their works being accepted for Christ's sake. That Christians are not totally depraved, see Berkhof, *Systematic Theology*, p. 246ff (by inference); Anthony A. Hoekema, *The Christian Looks at Himself* (Grand Rapids: Wm. B. Eerdmans Pub. Co., 1979), pp. 47-48.

[8] Though the aorist tense does not mean "once for all" in itself, it can if the context demands, and in Romans 6 the word "once for all" (*ephapax*) is used.

[9] We have not developed the doctrine of union with Christ though it is implied in

His death and resurrection, they partake of His position and grace in regard to the ruling power of sin in their lives: They died to sin once for all so that it cannot rule them (position or death to sin necessarily affects life).

Justification, therefore, is a legal act while sanctification is a moral work. Both are received simultaneously though sanctification is the effect of justification. A person either has both or neither, and both are merited by Jesus alone in His death and resurrection (Gal. 3:3).

What Is the Relationship of Sanctification to Obedience?

In this part of the review, we shall see how faith, growth, and works are related.

Relationship of Grace to Law

It is difficult to believe that the Reformed are accused of believing that sanctification is by obedience to the law, but this is what Robert Lightner, a professor of systematic theology at DTS, says: "[The Reformed] teach that while justification is by grace through faith, sanctification is by obedience to the law."[10] The reason may be that the Reformed emphasize the importance of obedience to God's commands to the point that if one does not obey, then he is not a Christian. This is precisely what Scripture says. But nowhere do either Scripture or the Reformed theologians state that obedience to the law gains us sanctification, but that we obey because we are being sanctified (Phil. 2:12-13). Let us confirm this even more.

From Ephesians 1, grace originates in the election of God the Father (1:4-6), is mediated through the Cross of Jesus (1:7-12), and is applied by the Holy Spirit (1:13-14).[11] At each "stage" God's grace is from Himself to man, with man having

---

what we have said. See John Murray in *Redemption Accomplished and Applied.*

[10]Robert Lightner, *Bibliotheca Sacra*, July-September, 1986, p. 234.

[11]In Ephesians 1:13-14 we have the sealing of the Spirit when one believes. It is not explicitly stated that the grace here is irresistible though it is implied in all that has gone before.

nothing to do to merit it. In Dillow's scheme, we would have grace coming from the Father, merited by the sinner's faith to obtain the merits of the Cross stored in a spiritual treasury,[12] and then merited by the saint's works to obtain the ministry of the Spirit. Such a concept violates the natural flow of the passage and introduces a sinner who has nothing to do with any of the work accomplished. From beginning (election) to end (glorification), salvation is the work of God: Father, Son, and Holy Spirit.

"For we are His workmanship, created in Christ Jesus *for* good works, which God prepared beforehand that we should walk in them" (Eph. 2:10). Does not this verse state that it is God's grace and purpose that gives us the ability to keep His commandments? Is not this irresistible grace for sanctification?

"You did not choose Me, but I chose you and appointed you that you should go and bear fruit, and *that your fruit should remain.* . . ." (John 15:16). According to this verse, what are the conditions for having fruit remain? It is the choosing of Christ, and all those He has chosen will have fruit or else they are cast out and burned (v. 6).

Philippians 2:12, 13 puts in perspective the relationship between our works and the grace of God: "Work out your own salvation with fear and trembling; for it is God who works in you both to will and to do for His good pleasure." Paul is not saying that we are to work *for* our salvation but that we are to live *out* what God works in us. The "for" of verse 13 explains how we can work out our salvation; it is because the grace of God first works in us to enable us to perform it.

Likewise in Romans 8:4, the Christian fulfills or obeys the law because God the Spirit enables him to do so: ". . . that the righteous requirement of the law might be fulfilled in us who

---

[12]If the merits of His death were not effectual in themselves, then like the Roman Catholic Church teaches they must be stored in a spiritual treasury somewhere until man "appropriates" them. The biblical teaching is that Christ's death guarantees the elect's faith rather than man's faith guaranteeing His death. In other words, Christ's death keeps man's faith from being a failure rather than man's faith keeping Christ's death from being a failure. Because His death is effectual (unlimited in quality), the elect will believe (limited in quantity). Calvinists teach that Jesus did everything for some while Arminians teach that Christ did something for every man.

do not walk according to the flesh but according to the Spirit." And we walk by the Spirit and live by the Spirit if the Spirit of God dwells in us (not by obeying some command); otherwise we are not His (v. 9). Thus the Spirit irresistibly enables us to live out the law, but those who are in the flesh cannot please God (vv. 7, 8), and they go to hell.

It should be clear, therefore, that the source of grace is not ourselves but God alone; and that this grace from God enables us to obey. Nor is it true that this grace only brings us to a point of neutrality, but as Calvin said on 1 John 3:9; grace rules our hearts.

Relationship of Grace to Fruit

As we have seen, grace for sanctification comes directly from God through the Cross (Titus 2:14; Eph. 5:25-27; 1:3-14). This grace is not "provided" for us to merit by our works through some sort of "appropriation." He is the *source*, enabling us to use the *means* for our growth, and this growth in turn produces certain *fruit* in our lives. Thus we have the logical order of source (grace), means (human effort), and effect (fruit).

This may be compared to our physical life. The cause or source of our physical life is from God alone (Acts 17:24-29). We cannot merit this, produce it, or lessen it. The means for our physical growth is eating food, exercise, and rest, but we would not use these means unless we were first alive. And all who are alive use the means, but if they never use the means, we would rightly conclude that there is no life. Then there are fruits in one's life, such as one becoming a great football player or some other physical feat, which are gained by using the means.

God the Holy Spirit applies the grace Christ gained for us; He is the source. He gives us life. We use the means to grow such as Bible study, church attendance, fellowship with other believers, prayer, suffering, and so on. From the source we use the means, from the means we produce fruit in our lives, some thirty fold, some sixty, and some a hundred — but all produce some.

Conclusion

Ryrie wrote a chapter in *Walvoord: A Tribute* claiming to

believe, like the Reformed, that justification and sanctification are inseparable,[13] but he has written hundreds of pages his whole life denying this. In *Balancing the Christian Life* he has a chart displaying his view, temporally separating sanctification from justification, beginning sanctification with the crisis dedication of Romans 12:1.[14] This is emphatically not the Reformed view. And eleven years later in *Walvoord: A Tribute*, he has not really changed his mind, beginning sanctification in dedication and continuing it in the filling of the Spirit, thus making sanctification conditioned on one's obedience. Once this is granted, it is obvious that he has made a temporal separation between them, making sanctification optional.

Like Dillow, Ryrie has never understood the Pelagian problem of whether grace engages our obedience or our obedience engages grace. In senior theology, Ryrie presented sanctification as beginning in dedication (Rom. 12:1), and after class I asked him if sanctification was not being done at all before the crisis dedication. Typically his response was double talk: "Well, I suppose in some sense it is, but you will not get very far without dedication." I then made my question as pungent and to the point as I could: "Does God's grace grant the dedication or does the dedication grant the grace?" More double talk: "They engage one another." Incredible. He has never understood the relationship of grace to law. In separating law as the produce of grace, we have separated sanctification from justification, giving regenerate man two separate natures resulting in two kinds of Christians, carnal and spiritual, a faith without works, and so on *ad nauseam*.

Dillow does not even claim as much as Ryrie, making sanctification completely separate from justification and conditioned on works, arguing this for many pages, even specifically stating many times that sanctification is by our works. Dillow is more consistent than Ryrie, but neither of them present the biblical relationship of justification to sanctification.

---

[13]Donald K. Campbell, *Walvoord: A Tribute* (Chicago: Moody Press, 1982), p. 193.

[14]Charles Caldwell Ryrie, *Balancing the Christian Life* (Chicago: Moody Press, 1971), p. 184.

Assurance of Faith

It is here that Dillow rages the most, charging that the Reformed have been inconsistent in both their views of faith and of assurance. He alleges that Calvin and the Heidelberg Catechism held that personal assurance was of the essence of saving faith and that none of the Reformed taught that faith included the will (pp. 283, 288). According to Dillow, one cannot have true faith and lack personal assurance, or if one lacks assurance he is not a Christian. But let us examine these assertions more closely.

Assurance and Dillow's Confusion

Dillow does not seem to understand the Reformed difference between objective and subjective assurance. His discussion of several chapters only gives a hint that he is aware of the interchange regarding these. Is assurance of the essence of faith? Yes and no. Objective assurance refers to a persuasion that the promises in the Gospel are true while subjective assurance refers to one knowing that he personally is a Christian. The Reformed from Calvin's day to ours have taught that saving faith includes a persuasion in the objective promises of the Gospel, for as Calvin rightly stated, how can one even be a Christian if he doubts that Jesus is God and man, that He died as our Substitute and arose bodily from the grave? In this objective aspect, assurance is of the essence of faith.

On the other hand, from Calvin through the Westminster divines, the Reformed, reflecting Scripture, have also taught that one may be a Christian and not have subjective assurance, the knowledge that he personally has an interest in Christ. In other words, one may be persuaded that he is a sinner and that Jesus is a great Savior (objective) and yet not be persuaded that he has been born again (subjective). Robert Shaw, in his exposition of the Westminster Confession of Faith entitled *The Reformed Faith* discusses these things (p. 181ff) as does George Gillespie in *The Works of George Gillespie* (vol. 2, p. 104ff). A very extensive and valuable discussion of the history of assurance is *Assurance of Faith: Calvin, English Puritanism, and the Dutch Second Reformation*, by Joel R. Beeke.[1] In this latter volume, Beeke cogently argues that Calvin, the Westminster divines, John Owen and subsequent Reformed theologians have maintained the objective and subjective nature of assurance, the exact statements varying according to the emphasis needed for the particular circumstances of the day. Indeed, the Reformed from Calvin to our day have consistently maintained three aspects to assurance: (1) objectively the truthfulness of the Gospel promises and subjectively (2) that the Holy Spirit convinces us that we are personally His (Rom. 8:16) and (3) that the fruit in our lives is His.

Consider these statements of the WCF: "This certainty is not a bare conjectural and probable persuasion, grounded upon a fallible hope; but an infallible assurance of faith, founded upon the divine truth of promises of salvation [objective], the inward evidence of those graces unto which these promises are made, the testimony of the Spirit of adoption witnessing with our spirits that we are the children of God [subjective]. . . ."[2] Thus for Dillow to rail for three chapters that the Reformed do not believe that assurance is of the essence of faith only reveals his ignorance in the objective/subjective distinction.

Dillow is adamant that fruit in one's life has nothing to do with assurance and so maintains for several chapters. One quote will suffice: ". . . there are no necessary actions of the will . . . or good works required to verify its [faith] presence"

---

[1]New York: Peter Lang: American University Studies, vol. 89, 1991. Must reading! William Cunningham's chapter "The Reformers and the Doctrine of Assurance" is also very informative in his book, *The Reformers and the Theology of the Reformation* (Edinburgh: The Banner of Truth Trust, 1862, 1979). His conclusions do not seem to be as well thought out as Beeke's though.

[2]WCF: 18.2.

(p. 284). To Dillow, if one requires works or change in one's life before personal (subjective) assurance can be had, he has added works to salvation. But how does one understand Dillow in other places where he says:

> This is not to deny that true faith certainly involves a disposition of openness to God and cannot coexist with an attitude of determination to continue in sin (p. 10).

> A man who claims he is a Christian and yet never manifests any change at all has no reason to believe he is justified (Mark 4:5, 16-17) (p. 21).

> ... we would have serious doubts about the salvation of a man who claims he is a Christian and gives little or no evidence of it in his life. We would not give assurance of salvation to such an individual (p. 23).[3]

We would ask Dillow the same questions he asks us, How much change must one have before he can be sure he is a Christian? Is this not looking to one's works as a part of assurance? Logic defies how these statements could be construed as meaning anything except that one cannot have assurance without fruit so that the problem he accuses the Reformed of having is his also! Apparently there is a possibility of self-deception, for Dillow says one can claim to be a Christian and yet be wrong. On the other hand, he argues for pages that one knows when he has believed so that self-deception is not possible. Which is it? He argues that one is self-aware when he believes that a president is trustworthy or when a tight rope walker may be trusted, but in these other quotes apparently one may not have self-awareness of faith.

Ryrie asks in his book, *So Great Salvation*, How much fruit one must have before one can conclude that he is a Christian? Quantification is only a perceived problem, though, for the fallacy Ryrie commits is covered in most elementary logic books and is called "the argument of the beard": If you cannot tell me how many whiskers it takes to make a beard, then there can be no beards. We can intuitively see that this is bad logic.

---

[3]Later Dillow correctly says that the Bible does not allow one believer to give another believer assurance (p. 307), though here he implies one can. Dillow's inconsistency with himself is a constant problem throughout his work.

We cannot state how many whiskers it takes to make a beard, and yet it is obvious that some men have them and others do not. Perhaps in some cases it may be difficult to state if a man has reached the "beard" stage or not. Likewise, it is obvious that some people are Christians and some are not while with others it is difficult to tell. Of course *God* infallibly knows those who are His.

Assurance and the Will

Dillow chastises MacArthur in his book, *The Gospel According to Jesus,* for saying that Reformed theologian Berkhof holds to faith as including a volitional aspect. Dillow wants faith to be understanding only, like the Roman Catholics, and void of *any* aspect of the will, and he cites Berkhof as agreeing with him against MacArthur that faith does not have a volitional aspect. How one can have trust without involving the will, Dillow does not explain, but that Berkhof means that faith includes the will that leads to obedience is easily seen from the very pages MacArthur and Dillow cite. In defining faith Berkhof says it includes:

> A *Volitional element*. This is the crowning element of faith. Faith is not merely a matter of the intellect, nor of the intellect and the emotions combined; it is also a matter of the will.[4]

> [James's] idea of the faith that justifies does not differ from that of Paul, but he stresses the fact that this faith must manifest itself in good works. If it does not, it is dead faith, and is, in fact, non-existent.[5]

Thus MacArthur was right in his understanding of Berkhof, and Dillow wrong. In contradiction to Dillow, Berkhof states:

> Antinomians . . . regarded faith simply as an intellectual acceptance. . . .[6]

Regarding the necessity of good works, Berkhof is again against Dillow:

---

[4]*Systematic Theology*, p. 505.

[5]Ibid., p. 499.

[6]Ibid., p. 508.

[Good works are] the fruits of faith. Antinomians . . . claim that . . . the believer is free from the obligation to observe [the law], an error that is still with us today in . . . dispensationalism.[7]

Dillow's definition of faith is that it is "located in the mind and is persuasion or belief" and "the will plays no part" (p. 276). Thus we have a type of fideism, one believing he is saved because he believes his faith is genuine because he believes his belief in his faith is real, an infinite regression. In the Reformed position, one's faith is directed to Christ and the Gospel, indeed the whole Trinity.[8] One's faith is directed out of himself to God, but in Dillow's view faith become its own object. In the Reformed view, one's faith is confirmed by the internal testimony of the Holy Spirit and the fruit in one's life, whereas Dillow teaches that these are not necessary.

In the Reformed concept, a lack of personal assurance causes one to run to the Triune God and use the means of grace, *looking to Christ for confirmation, to produce in him graces that he cannot produce himself,* whereas Dillow would say one is lost if he lacks personal assurance for *it is of the essence of faith.* Dillow complains that the Reformed view of faith causes consternation in believers who sometimes struggle to know if they are Christians, but in his view a believer would be in abject despair, as doubts unequivocally indicate that he does not have saving faith at all. With the Reformed, one is in union with Christ so that His grace is continually supplying the saint with the ability to produce good works by the Holy Spirit, whereas Dillow has the saint producing works independently of the Holy Spirit, or at least the saint must work first to *allow* the Holy Spirit to work. The Reformed do not believe that our works ever merit anything but that they are produced in us by the Holy Spirit, but Dillow says "we come to know Him in a deeper sense by means of obedience" (p. 165) and that our works "are meritorious" (p. 275). In this latter quote, Dillow says our works are co-produced by the Spirit and us, but they still are meritorious, making God our debtor.

---

[7]Ibid., p. 543. Dillow is a dispensationalist, and antinomianism tends to be part of their system. See appendix 3.

[8]See John Owen's volume 2.

Pastorally, should one who is living in disobedience have personal assurance? Conversely, should not one who has been changed have encouragement that God is at work in his life? Once I was teaching Greek in my home to a doctor, a business man, and a college student. The student through tears of joy spoke of his *former* (see 1 Cor. 6:11) homosexual lifestyle. He said that he knew he was truly converted when he saw a nude male and did not desire him. But according to Dillow, this potentially meant nothing. He says that though our works may bring "secondary encouragement" (the Reformed position!), yet "when absent they prove nothing" (p. 252, antinomian). In other words, this man could have continued in his sinful lifestyle, and this should not have affected his assurance at all. Even further, for a man who continues in sin to have personal assurance would be *to encourage a hypocrite and confirm him to hell, which is the real danger of this license theology.* One who is living in sin is not supposed to have personal assurance, for this is part of God's discipline to bring him back in line. The preacher who encourages assurance to such a one will have his blood on his hands and will be severely judged.

Dillow thinks one can have perfect personal assurance, but this is not possible unless one can have perfect faith. And if one cannot be sinless in this life (and he cannot), then he cannot have perfect faith.

Dillow screams that the Reformed encourage a syllogism to have assurance since they include the will in faith and make works an effect of faith, but he also must use a syllogism unless he believes it is impossible for one to be self-deceived. A syllogism is a conclusion drawn from the statements of Scripture that is not specifically stated by Scripture. Therefore, since the Bible nowhere says that John Doe is justified, he must reach this conclusion by taking an inference from the evidence given in Scripture (see notes on 1 John below). If one believes, he is converted. I believe, therefore I am converted. I know that I have faith by His effects of grace in my life. Therefore, it is quite impossible not to use logic.

Assurance, John Calvin, and Westminster

Dillow has not understood Calvin. He accuses Calvin of holding to a faith devoid of works and of a faith including the essence of personal assurance. While Calvin does speak this way of assurance, the enemy he was facing was the Roman Catholic Church which taught that personal assurance was either impossible or only by special revelation from God. The enemy at that time was legalism. The later Puritans and Westminster divines believed as Calvin that objective assurance was of the essence of faith, but had a new enemy: antinomianism. *Therefore while Calvin emphasized the objective side of assurance, the later divines emphasized the subjective side, though both Calvin and the subsequent theologians held to both sides.* There is a beautiful balance to the doctrine of assurance, for to hold only to the objective side leads to antinomianism and to maintain only the subjective side leads to legalism. We shall see both sides of assurance confirmed in the following quotes from both Calvin and the later divines. Stipulating that Calvin held to objective assurance as contained in the nature of faith, we shall also see that he knew that personal assurance could be doubted:

> [On 1 John 2:3] He [John] hence concludes, that they by no means know God who keep not his precepts or commandments. . . . obedience is so connected with knowledge, that the last is yet in order the first, as the cause is necessarily before its effect. But we are not hence to conclude that faith recumbs on works; for though every one receives a testimony to his faith from his works, yet it does not follow that it is founded on them, since they are added as an evidence. Then the certainty of faith depends on the grace of Christ alone; but piety and holiness of life distinguish true faith from that knowledge of God which is fictitious and dead; for the truth is, that those who are in Christ, as Paul says, have put off the old man (Col. 3:9).[9]

---

[9]John Calvin, *Calvin's Commentaries*, vol. 22 (Grand Rapids: Baker Book House, 1979), pp. 174, 175.

There are very many who so conceive God's mercy that they receive almost no consolation from it. They are constrained with miserable anxiety at the same time as they are in doubt whether he will be merciful to them. . . .[10]

Surely, while we teach that faith ought to be certain and assured, we cannot imagine any certainty that is not tinged with doubt, or any assurance that is not assailed by some anxiety.[11]

Therefore the godly heart feels in itself a division because it is partly imbued with sweetness from its recognition of the divine goodness, partly grieves in bitterness from an awareness of its calamity; partly rests upon the promise of the Gospel, partly trembles at the evidence of its own iniquity; partly rejoices at the expectation of life, partly shudders at death. This variation arises from imperfection of faith, since in the course of the present life it never goes so well with us that we are wholly cured of the disease of unbelief and entirely filled and possessed by faith.[12]

. . . the faithful are taught to examine themselves with solicitude and humility, lest carnal security insinuate itself, instead of the assurance of faith.[13]

Hence let us learn to examine ourselves, and to search whether those interior marks by which God distinguishes his children from strangers belong to us, viz., the living root of piety and faith.[14]

The Spirit of God gives us such a testimony, that when he is our guide and teacher our spirit is made sure of the adoption of God; for our mind of itself, without the preceding testimony of the Spirit, could not convey to us this assurance.[15]

---

[10]John Calvin, *Institutes of the Christian Religion* (Philadelphia: The Westminster Press, 1975), 3.2.15.

[11]Ibid., 3.2.17.

[12]Ibid., 3.2.18.

[13]Ibid., 3.2.7.

[14]Commentary on Ezekiel 13:9.

[15]Commentary on Romans 8:16.

Thus we can see that Dillow is dead wrong about Calvin's view of faith and assurance. Dillow quotes Calvin where he holds that objective assurance is of the essence of faith and concludes that this was the sum total of his view, not realizing that one could hold to both the objective and subjective aspects. If Dillow had read more widely in Reformed literature, he would have seen that though some Reformed theologians say that Calvin held only to the objective side yet others rightly see that this was not true. As Berkhof accurately summarizes:

> The Reformers . . . stressed assurance one-sidedly as the most important element of faith. . . . Yet it is quite evident . . . (a) that they did not meant to teach that this trust did not include other elements; and (b) that they did not intend to deny that true children of God must frequently struggle with all kinds of doubts and uncertainties.[16]

Berkhof further states that the "Antinomians considered this assurance to be the whole essence of faith. They ignored all other activities of faith, and regarded faith simply as an intellectual acceptance of the proposition: Thy sins are forgiven thee."[17] We could substitute the name Dillow for antinomians in this quote.

Dillow seems to say that we know we are justified by the power of the human mind as seen in the nature of faith whereas Calvin and the Reformed (p. 249) say that the Holy Spirit is the One who convinces us that we are His. It is not that the Reformed say that the Holy Spirit by some mysticism convinces us that we belong to Jesus but that by the internal process of sanctification He does so.

Likewise, the Westminster Divines and the Puritans held to both aspects of assurance. (The reader is referred to Beeke's book, especially chapter 18, in which he demonstrates that these divines held to both aspects.) Therefore, the WCF could say that assurance is "founded upon the divine truth of the promises of salvation" (18.2) meaning objectively so and yet also maintain that assurance "doth not *so* belong to the

---

[16]*Systematic Theology*, p. 507.

[17]Ibid., p. 508.

essence of faith" (18.3) without contradiction. Indeed, the word "so," according to Thomas Boston (1676-1732), meant that objective assurance did indeed belong to the essence of faith but personal assurance did not. He comments: "How faith can grow in any to a full[18] assurance, if there be no assurance in the nature of it, I cannot comprehend."[19] Indeed, As Beeke points out, the WCF on assurance is summarized as follows: the *possibility* of assurance (18.1), the *foundation* of assurance (18.2), the *cultivation* of assurance (18.3), and the *renewal* of assurance (18.4).[20] Nowhere does the WCF affirm assurance by looking at oneself apart from the Gospel promises, as Dillow falsely accuses. Beeke marshals many quotes from Puritan divines that demonstrate this agreement with the first Reformers, only their emphasis was on the subjective part because of the new enemy of antinomianism. Francis Turretin (1623-87) stated:

> By the direct act man believes the promises of the Gospel: while by the reflex he looking upon his faith knows that he believes. The direct act precedes, the reflex follows, and such a subordination exists between them, that just as the direct draws the reflex after it, so the reflex necessarily supposes the first, nor has it a place unless the direct has gone before. . . .[21]

George Gillespie (1613-1649), highly influential at the Westminster Assembly, grants encouragement to those for whom Christ died.[22]

William Perkins (1558-1602), who greatly influenced the Westminster divines, said that both the strengths (by the grace of God) and weaknesses (indwelling sins) serve to drive believers to Christ "that they might be *all in all* out of themselves in Christ."[23] To this Beeke insightfully adds:

---

[18]The divines often used "full" assurance to mean not only objective but also personal assurance.

[19]Beeke, *Assurance of Faith*, p. 174.

[20]Ibid., p. 147.

[21]Ibid., p. 162.

[22]George Gillespie, *The Works of George Gillespie* (Edmonton: Still Waters Revival Books, 1644, 1991), p. 117ff.

[23]Beeke, *Assurance of Faith*, p. 168.

"There could be no better defusing of the objective-subjective tension in assurance than this!" Furthermore, Beeke establishes that Perkins held that assurance rests on three principles: the general promise of the Gospel, the testimony of the Holy Spirit, and the syllogism or reflex part of faith that rests partly on the Gospel and partly on experience.[24] Thus Perkins held to both the objective and subjective aspects of assurance, and, as the Reformed men have held, the subjective part rises out of the objective. One's fruits are not to be considered apart from the promises of the Gospel as if one could have works without faith, or fruit without the Holy Spirit.

Samuel Rutherford (1660-1661) proclaims:

> The germ of assurance is surely implicit in the salvation which the believer comes to possess by faith, it is implicit in the change that has been wrought in his state and condition. . . . At the lowest ebb of faith and hope and love his consciousness never drops to the level of the unbeliever at its highest pitch of confidence and assurance.[25]

John Owen (1616-1683), who did not take part in the WCF, was still regarded by many as a divine who had much influence over the WCF and as the greatest English theologian of his day. (He is still the greatest!) Owen, who wrote the Savoy Declaration of Faith and Order (1658), used the WCF as the basic guide, changing only some words in a few parts. On assurance he changed the WCF to read more specifically as follows:

> This certainty is not a bare conjectural and probable persuasion, grounded upon a fallible hope, but an infallible assurance of faith, founded *on the blood and righteousness of Christ, revealed in the Gospel, and also upon* the inward evidence of those graces unto which promises are made, *and on the immediate witness* of the Spirit, *testifying our adoption, and as a fruit thereof, leaving the heart more humble and holy.*[26]
> [The words in italics reveal his changes from the WCF.]

---

[24]Ibid., p. 108.

[25]Ibid., p. 189.

[26]Ibid., p. 237.

The reader should note that the words "and also upon" reveal that Owen held to both objective and subjective in assurance, and in agreement with all the Reformed divines grounds the subjective in the objective.

As we can see, the Reformed most emphatically do not ground their personal assurance on their works, contrary to Dillow, but on the objective work of Christ. When the saint is without works, he must renew his commitment by running again to Jesus, using the means of grace, looking to Him to produce in himself what he cannot do. When again the evidence is there, he does not look to it but to the One Who gave it, realizing that it came from Him. How, in the name of all that is biblical and rational, is this full assurance said to be *grounded* on works when the works are the fruits? If one is adopted into a rich family from a poor one and given a Mercedes, does he conclude that he earned the Mercedes? Does he ground his adoption on the Mercedes, saying that it is the reason he knows he is adopted, or is the adoption grounded in the grace of the parents, the Mercedes being the evidence? Yet if he is without any evidence of his sonship, if nothing has changed in his life, if he still lives in poverty, should he not conclude that his adoption is a myth?[27]

Assurance and Commands to Examine Ourselves

We shall only give a few responses to Dillow's concept that we do not need to examine ourselves, not the least of which is that some saints in Scripture lacked assurance:

> For I said in my haste, "I am cut off from before Your eyes"; Nevertheless You heard the voice of my supplications When I cried out to You (Ps. 31:22, David).

> In the day of my trouble I sought the Lord; my hand was stretched out in the night without ceasing; my soul refused to be comforted (Ps. 77:2, Solomon).

---

[27]This is based on the logical form: If A, then B; if not B, then not A. If adopted, then good works. If not good works, then not adopted.

Romans 8:16

Since Calvin, this verse has been used by the Reformed in the assurance of salvation. The fact that Dillow does not even mention Romans 8:16 in his chapters on assurance implies that he has not read much in the Reformed writings on assurance, or if he has he overlooked a major point. The exegetical question is what is the *"witness* of the Spirit"? Divines have differed over whether the witness is immediate or mediate (directly to the person or indirectly).[28]

John Murray labors hard to demonstrate that the verb for "bear witness" always involves two witnesses,[29] and so here the Spirit along with our spirits enables us to reach the conclusion that we are God's children. In context the "witness of the Spirit" is done along with "walking according to the Spirit" (vv. 4-5), being "in the Spirit" (v. 9), "putting to death the deeds of the body" (v. 13), and "being led by the Spirit" (v. 14), all of which are terms for sanctification. The latter expression is used in Galatians 5:18 of being led in the sense of sanctification. Indeed, Warfield concludes that the "leading" is a virtual synonym for sanctification.[30] This meaning of "leading" fits the Romans context well where the one who "walks according to the Spirit" is not carnally minded (vv. 4-8) but is "in the Spirit," which is true of all Christians: "But you are not in the flesh but *in the Spirit,* if indeed the Spirit of God dwells in you. Now if anyone does not have the Spirit of Christ, he is not His" (v. 9). The one who is "in the Spirit" is also "putting to death the deeds of the body" (v. 13) as he is "being led by the Spirit" (v. 14) into further sanctification. In light of such working by the Spirit in the believer's life, Paul says we have "received the Spirit of adoption" who "bears witness with our spirit" that we are His. This bearing witness,

---

[28]Thomas Goodwin held to the immediate witness as did C. E. S. Cranfield, *International Critical Commentary: Romans* (Edinburgh: T. & T. Clark, 1977), 1:402. For the majority Reformed view, see John Murray, *The Epistle to the Romans* (Grand Rapids: Wm. B. Eerdmans Pub. Co., 1975), 1:297 and especially *The Collected Writings of John Murray* (Edinburgh: The Banner of Truth Trust, 1977), 1:186ff, 2:272ff.

[29]*Collected Writings*, 1:186ff.

[30]By all means read Warfield's most excellent article on Romans 8:14 in *Biblical and Theological Studies*, p. 543ff!

therefore, has to do with the resultant progress in one's life, his victory over sin, which is a means of personal assurance.

Finally, if personal assurance is of the essence of faith, as Dillow maintains, then we do not need this verse. Apparently, Paul disagreed, thinking that we need this ministry of the Spirit added to our faith to reach personal assurance.

2 Peter 1:10

The verse reads: "Therefore, brethren, be even more diligent to make your calling and election sure, for if you do these things you will never stumble." It would seem that words could not be clearer that one is to make sure of his election by using the means, and Peter has just listed several character qualities that we must cultivate in our lives by the power of the Spirit (vv. 5-7). He who lacks these things "has forgotten that he was cleansed from his old sins" (v. 9), and to him who has them "an entrance will be supplied . . . abundantly[31] into the everlasting kingdom of our Lord and Savior, Jesus Christ" (v. 11).

Of course, Dillow relies on his disparity hermeneutic to find myriad distinctions where none exist. First, he says that the word for "sure" ("make your calling . . . *sure*") does not mean something subjective in one's heart in other New Testament passages, which is against his own hermeneutic of taking the semantic value of a word only in its immediate context. Furthermore, the Arndt and Gingrich Greek lexicon lists many places where he is unequivocally wrong.[32] Peter is writing to Christians, Dillow says, so he could not be in doubt of their "salvation."[33] This is a theological hermeneutic based on the analogy of faith, for Dillow has concluded from other passages that one cannot lose his justification. In this context he refers to "calling" and "cleansed" to confirm that they are Christians (p. 297). Dillow's analogy of faith application is wrong, for as we have said before one can be in covenant with God and not necessarily be regenerated, though the same

[31]"Abundantly" does not imply some enter but just not abundantly, but simply means "richly."

[32]p. 138, 2nd ed.

[33]Does Dillow mean justification or sanctification or both, as Peter does?

terms are used. What Peter does say — and Dillow cannot erase it — is that we must make our election sure. Peter does not say to determine our election — only God can do that. If we make it sure, what is this but assurance?

2 Corinthians 13:5

"Examine yourselves as to whether you are in the faith. Prove yourselves. Do you not know yourselves, that Jesus Christ is in you? — unless indeed you are disqualified." Once again it is difficult to imagine a stronger verse, and if we are to examine ourselves, then personal assurance is not of the essence of faith. Dillow uses the argument that "in the faith" is never used of possession of faith (p. 300) but of living right. (What is the difference?) This is an irrelevant statement if salvation cannot be divided. Furthermore, he is not using the semantic value of the phrase but the analogy of faith. Also, "in the faith" means "continue in the faith" (Col. 2:7), "established in the faith" (Col 2:7), "boldness in the faith" (1 Tim. 3:13, no article), "sound in the faith" (Titus 1:13), and "steadfast in the faith" (1 Peter 5:9). In these examples certain qualities of faith are given, some being the qualities of faith itself and others being the faith they believed. Consistent with this Paul challenges the Corinthians to confirm his apostleship by seeing if his preaching has indeed given them Christ, that Christ is in them, unless they fail the test. If they fail, they are non-Christians.

To relieve all doubt that Paul speaks of questioning their justification, he uses the word so often used in the epistles of this: "approved" or "disapproved."[34] The basic meaning of the word is to be tried, tested, and found to be genuine. Just note these examples:

> Each one's work will become manifest; for the Day will declare it, because it will be revealed by fire; and the fire will *test* each one's work, of what sort it is (1 Cor. 3:13).

> But I discipline my body and bring it into subjection, lest, when I have preached to others, I myself should become *disqualified* (1 Cor. 9:27).

---

[34]δοκιμαζω, αδοκιμος, δοκιμος. See G. Adolf Deissmann, *Bible Studies*, p. 259ff for a good study.

For there must also be factions among you, that those who are *approved* may be recognized among you (1 Cor. 11:19).

For not he who commends himself is *approved*, but whom the Lord commends (2 Cor. 10:18).

Examine yourselves as to whether you are in the faith. *Prove* yourselves. Do you not know yourselves, that Jesus Christ is in you? — unless indeed you are *disqualified*. But I trust that you will know that we are not *disqualified*. Now I pray to God that you do no evil, not that we should appear *approved*, but that you should do what is honorable, though we may seem *disqualified* (2 Cor. 13:5-7).

But as we have been *approved* by God to be entrusted with the Gospel, even so we speak, not as pleasing men, but God who *tests* our hearts (1 Thess. 2:4).

Now as Jannes and Jambres resisted Moses, so do these also resist the truth: men of corrupt minds, *disapproved* concerning the faith (2 Tim. 3:8).

They profess to know God, but in works they deny Him, being abominable, disobedient, and *disqualified* for every good work (Titus 1:16).

Blessed is the man who perseveres under trial; for when he has been *approved*, he will receive the crown of life which the Lord has promised to those who love Him (James 1:12).[35]

That the *genuineness* of your faith, being much more precious than gold that perishes, though it is *tested* by fire, may be found to praise, honor, and glory at the revelation of Jesus Christ (1 Peter 1:7).

So much for Dillow's argument.

1 John

Tests in 1 John

Dillow says of the Reformed that they look to the tests in 1 John as "tests of whether or not a man is truly born again. . . . The believer is commanded to look within, to fruits

---

[35]My translation.

in the life, and not to Christ to examine the basis for his justification" (p. 157). Again Dillow has erected a straw man. Though the Reformed do use the tests of 1 John, they most emphatically teach to look to Christ. And what does he mean by "examine the *basis* for his justification"? Does he mean the "supporting factor" or the "foundation"? No Reformed theologian in the history of the world has ever declared that the *foundation* for his justification is his fruits but Christ alone, and fruit is a "supporting factor" if we mean evidence and not cause. As we have seen, assurance has two sides, the objective side and the subjective side. The objective side is seen in 1 John 1:7-10; 3:23; 4:1-6, 14-16; 5:1, 10-12; the subjective in 1 John 2:3-5, 29; 4:7-11; and both in 1 John 3:4-15. It is not that John consciously decided to divide assurance in two parts, for one leads to the other. We can analyze assurance into its parts, like we can salvation, but they really go together. If one really knows Jesus, he will practice the commands of God (2:3-5). Conversely, if he does not practice His commands, he does not know Him (3:7-9). For full assurance one must objectively believe the right things about Jesus (4:1-6; 5:1, 10-12) and subjectively practice love for the brethren (4:7-11) and keep His commands (2:3-5). If one lacks this assurance, he must examine himself to see if he truly believes the promises of the Gospel, that Jesus is God and man who died as the substitute for his sins and was raised bodily from the grave. If he still lacks assurance, he must pursue the means of grace until God bears witness with his spirit that he is His. Thus the Christian looks primarily to Christ and the Gospel for assurance and only in a confirming sense to the fruit in his life.

Dillow versus 1 John

First John has suffered immeasurably from the hands of the antinomians. Dillow uses three methods to evade the trenchant statements of 1 John. First, he says that since the book is addressed to Christians (p. 157), we must interpret everything accordingly. We have dealt with this earlier; suffice it to say that once again he *assumes* that a book addressed to Christians cannot give them warnings regarding their salvation or that they cannot be covenant members and not converted, which is false.

Secondly, he develops an elaborate theory of gnosticism that threatened the early church, against which John wrote. I have little doubt that there is some truth in this, but how much has never been decided and how it tempers one's interpretation would have to been hammered out from specific passages. But Dillow himself falls into a gnosticism by holding that knowing is having (p. 276), or as Warfield stated, "Here, you see, is a truly rampant intellectualism, a pure gnosticism. To understand is to have and to be. In proportion as we understand, and understand intelligently, we possess."[36] According to Dillow, if one knows propositions, he automatically has Christ and assurance. As important as knowledge is, one must not stop there in his view of faith.

Thirdly, Dillow says the purpose of the book is revealed in the closing chapter: "These things I have written to you who believe in the name of the Son of God, that you may know that you have eternal life, and that you may [continue to] believe in the name of the Son of God" (1 John 5:13). With this we agree, for John similarly reveals his purpose in writing John toward the close of his Gospel.[37] The Gospel was written so that we may *have* eternal life (John 20:30-31) and 1 John so that we may *know* that we have eternal life. This is very balanced! The contention comes when Dillow says that 1 John was written and the tests designed to reveal whether we have *abundant* life (p. 162), not life itself. Again we have the second work of grace concept, the optional nature of sanctification, resistible grace, optional fruit in one's life, and just plain nonsense when one considers John's statements.

That salvation is a unit in 1 John can be seen not only from the whole book, but especially from 1 John 3:2-3:

> Beloved, now we are children of God [justification, saved from the penalty of sin]; and it has not yet been revealed what we shall be, but we know that when He is revealed, we shall be like Him, for we shall see Him as He is [glorification, will

---

[36]B. B. Warfield, *Counterfeit Miracles* (London: Banner of Truth Trust, 1918, 1972), pp. 219, 220.

[37]See the commentaries for striking similarities between John and 1 John, but I suggest a few: light and darkness, present tense regarding sinning, born again, Jesus' incarnation, mutual abiding, believing in Jesus, Jesus called the Word, and so forth.

be saved from the presence of sin]. And everyone who has this hope in Him purifies himself, just as He is pure [sanctification, being saved from the power of sin].

Is it not obvious that for John one either has all three tenses or none?

Furthermore, Dillow finds John's understanding of the tests in 1:3: ". . . that you also may have *fellowship* with us; and truly our *fellowship* is with the Father and with His Son Jesus Christ." The key word for Dillow is "fellowship," which allegedly does not refer to "entrance into eternal life at justification but to the continuing experience with Christ called fellowship. . . . In other words, we come to know Him in a deeper sense by means of obedience" (p. 164). Absolutely incredible! Notice the heresy that one's works are meritorious and give us more of God. With Dillow the "knowing" in 1 John is a deeper knowledge in sanctification and the "fellowship" is optional communion with God.

"Knowing God" in 1 John

"Knowing God" in 1 John, according to Dillow, does not mean to know in the justifying sense of forgiveness of sins but in the sanctifying sense of communion, as if the two are separable. Dillow justifies this farce with an appeal — not to 1 John — to the analogy of faith in John where Philip is addressed by Jesus: "If you had known Me, you would have known My Father also; and from now on you know Him and have seen Him." According to Dillow, Philip already knew Jesus in a saving sense but not in a deeper sense (p. 164). But Philip's failure to pay attention to the Lord's revelation of the Father does not mean that by works he would come to know the Father in a deeper sense or that this is what "know" means in every context in 1 John. Dillow responds, "Knowing God is a matter of degrees, while being born again . . . is an absolute transition from hell to heaven" (p. 165). This can be true, though rarely, but is this what John means by "know"? We shall see below.

Dillow's second argument is that John equates "knowing God" with "abiding in Him (2:6)" (p. 164), and since abiding is supposedly optional, then "knowing Him" is optional in the deeper sense. This deeper sense is "knowing God" in sanctification, not in justification.[38] Dillow believes in a relationship that may not include fellowship, a position without practice, a Christian who may be in the darkness and still be born again, and so on.

Regarding "knowing God," in 2:3-5 is John saying that our works reveal if we know Him deeply or if we know Him at all? Is "knowing" quantitative or qualitative in 1 John? We can answer this by observing other terms used around "knowing God": the one who does not keep His commands does not know Him and the truth does not abide in him (2:4); those who know Him are "in Him" (2:5); sins forgiven (2:12-13); knowing the Son includes knowing the Father (2:23); the world does not know Him but Christians do (3:1-2); the one who knows Him (3:6) has had his sins taken away (3:7) and is a child of God (3:10) while the others are children of the devil (3:10); knowing God (4:6) means that Christians listen to the truth in contrast to the false prophets (4:1); the one who knows God loves the brethren and has been born again (4:7-8); and we know the Father through the Son (5:20). In each case the "knowing" is not optional or something deeper; it is absolute and qualitative.

"Fellowship" in 1 John

The word "fellowship" does not mean simply optional communication with God. It is a participation in something. Arndt and Gingrich define it as a "close relationship"[39] giving many passages as proofs (1 Cor. 1:9; 2 Cor. 6:14; 13:13; Phil. 2:1; Rom. 15:26, and 1 John 1:3b, 6). "Fellowship" in 1 John 1 means a relationship that includes communion, which has been the view of almost everyone except a few dispensationalists:

> [In 1 John fellowship describes] the living bond in which the Christian stands. Here, too, the word implies inward fellowship on a religious basis. To be a Christian is to have fellowship with God. . . . The believer's communion with God or Christ consists in mutual abiding (1 John 3:24; 4:13), which begins in this world and reaches into the world to come, where

---

[38] See appendix 1 for a refutation of the antinomian concept of "abiding."

[39] 2nd ed., p. 438.

it finds its supreme fulfillment (3:2).[40]

. . . that which distinguishes peculiarly Christians rather than simply that which they enjoy. . . the Gospel of which the end was to create spiritual fellowship between God and man and men. . . .[41]

The most terrible delusion results when this fact regarding God is in any way ignored when we consider our fellowship . . . or communion with God. To think that we can remain in darkness and yet be in fellowship with Him in whom there is no darkness whatever is the height of delusion. . . It is . . . axiomatic: "What communion has light with darkness? (2 Cor. 6:14; 1 John 3:19-21)."[42]

It is a fellowship which commits the child of God to a life of holiness as Paul says in 2 Cor. 6:14.[43]

[The true life in man which comes through acceptance of Jesus as Son of God.][44]

[Same as Philippians 1:5; 2:1; Philemon 6.][45]

True believers are those who dwell in Christ. . . . it is the fellowship into which believers are introduced and in which they are maintained by the indwelling Spirit of Christ.[46]

. . . consists in the fact that Christians are partakers in common

---

[40]Gerhard Kittel, *Theological Dictionary of the New Testament* (Grand Rapids: Wm. B. Eerdmans Pub. Co., 1972), 3:807-08.

[41]B. F. Westcott, *The Epistles of St. John* (Grand Rapids: Wm. B. Eerdmans Pub. Co., 1966), pp. 12-13.

[42]R. C. H. Lenski, *The Interpretation of 1 & 2 Peter, the Three Epistles of John. . . .* (Minneapolis: Augsburg Pub. House, 1966), p. 383. Lenski means relationship by the word "fellowship."

[43]Alexander Ross, NIC series, *The Epistles of James and John* (Grand Rapids: Wm. B. Eerdmans Pub. Co., 1974), p. 138.

[44]Marvin R. Vincent, *Word Studies in the New Testament* (Grand Rapids: Wm. B. Eerdmans Pub. Co., 1969), 2:309.

[45]Rudolph Bultmann, *The Johannine Epistles* (Philadelphia: Fortress Press, 1973), p. 12. We do not believe that Bultmann's theology is generally reliable.

[46]F. F. Bruce, *The Epistles of John* (Old Tappan, NJ: Fleming H. Revell Co., 1970), p. 39.

of the same mind as God and Christ, and of the blessings arising therefrom.[47]

Furthermore, the words used around "fellowship" indicate that John means a relationship involving communion — not optional communion. We have "eternal life" (v. 2), being cleansed by the blood of Christ (v. 7), and forgiveness of sins (v. 9), which in virtually all other contexts in the New Testament involves a relationship.

In his epistle John is not comparing degrees of fellowship or communion or sanctification but contrasting opposites: light versus darkness, truth versus error, sin versus righteousness, abiding versus not abiding, and in each case the contrast is absolute: a believer versus an unbeliever. There is no jumping back and forth between these spheres in John. Either a believer is in the light or an unbeliever in the darkness, and never is a believer in John spoken of as in the darkness. Consider John's usage:

> Then Jesus spoke to them again, saying, "I am the light of the world. *He who follows*[48] *Me shall not walk in darkness, but have the light of life*" (John 8:12).

> Then Jesus said to them, "A little while longer the light is with you. Walk while you have the light, lest darkness overtake you; he who walks in darkness does not know where he is going. While you have the light, believe in the light, that you may become sons of light." These things Jesus spoke, and departed, and was hidden from them. "I have come as a light into the world, that *whoever believes in Me should not abide in darkness*" (John 12:35-36, 46).

> But if we walk in the light as He is in the light, we have fellowship with one another, and the blood of Jesus Christ His Son cleanses us from all sin (1 John 1:7).

---

[47]Thayer's Greek lexicon, p. 352.

[48]The Greek word for "follow" in the Gospels often refers to being a disciple of Jesus; see these in John: 1:37, 43; 8:12; 10:4, 5, 27; 12:26; 21:20, 22; Rev. 14:4. In the Gospels one can be a disciple without being a Christian (John 6:66), but he cannot be a Christian without being a disciple (Luke 14:25ff ["Coming to Jesus," as we have seen, means coming Him for forgiveness]; John 2:11, 22; 6:44, 45, 66; 8:31ff, 15:8). In Acts a disciple and a Christian are identical (1:15; 6:1, 2, 7; *11:26*; 13:52).

And this is the condemnation, that the light has come into the world, and men loved darkness rather than light, because their deeds were evil. For everyone practicing evil hates the light and does not come to the light, lest his deeds should be exposed. But he who does the truth comes to the light, that his deeds may be clearly seen, that they have been done in God (John 3:19-21).

Thus in 1 John 1 when John speaks of "fellowship" in the light and others being in the darkness, he is contrasting opposites, not giving degrees of communion.

Furthermore, if one will study John's technical use of the prepositions *of* and *in*,[49] which has been noticed by more than one grammarian,[50] he will find that *of* often indicates ultimate source or identification and *in* the ultimate sphere of operation. For example, we are to be spatially *in* the world (John 17:11, 15) but not morally *of* the world (John 17:14, 16; 1 John 4:5). To be "in the truth" and "to have the truth" are often the same (1 John 1:8; 2:4 with 1 John 3:18; 2 John 2 with verse 4; 3 John 3-4). Everyone *of* the truth hears Jesus or listens to Him (John 18:37; 8:47; 10:26-27). Thus being *in* or *of* the light is a Christian, but being *in* or *of* darkness is a non-Christian.

In 1 John "knowing the truth" is salvation (primarily justification, John 8:32; 1 John 2:21; 2 John 1). To be "in sin" is to be enslaved and unforgiven (John 8:21, 24; 9:34) and to "have sin" emphasizes one's guilt (John 9:41; 15:22, 24; 19:11; 1 John 1:8).

That John uses present tenses with special significance is well known, especially with some verbs. "Doing (*poieo*) sin" is often the same as "sinning" (*harmartano*), indicating an unbeliever who is enslaved (John 8:34; 1 John 3:4, 6, 8; 5:18). By contrast John used the aorist tense of a Christian who commits an act of sin (1 John 2:1). Therefore, in 1 John 1 *in* the light and "not practicing (present tense) the truth" are abso-

---

[49]Greek is εκ, εν.

[50]Nigel Turner, *A Grammar of New Testament Greek* (Edinburgh: T. & T. Clark, 1963), vol. 3, pp. 260-263; Vol. 4, p. 76; Maximillan Zerwick, *Biblical Greek* (Rome: Biblical Institute Press, 1963), #134-5; Nigel Turner, *Grammatical Insights Into the New Testament* (Edinburgh: T. & T. Clark, 1965), p. 120; A. T. Robertson, *Word Pictures in the New Testament* (Nashville: Broadman Press, 1932), vol. 5, p. 57.

lutes. Also by John's consistent usage "His word not in us" and "the truth not in us" indicate non-Christians, not lower tier Christians who are not in of "fellowship" with Him.

Finally, many have noted the similarity between 1 John 1 and Romans 3, both speaking of justification before God, not simply of an "in and out" fellowship.[51] While Paul emphasizes primarily the legal aspect, John has both justification and sanctification in view. Notice this chart:

	Romans 3-4	1 John 1:1-2:2
All guilty before God	3:10-19	1:6, 8, 10
He is our propitiation	3:25	2:2
God is just and justifier	3:26	1:9
Relationship based on His blood	3:26	1:7
Justified	4:5-8	1:9
Faith alone	4:1-8	1:9

Even 1 John 1:9 is justification, not an optional communion. Many see 1 John 1:9 as acquittal and verse 7 as removal of sin.[52] Someone may object that one does not confess his sins to become a Christian ("If we confess our sins. . . ."), but he confesses the Son (Rom. 10:9-10). This is a half truth, for in confessing Jesus as Lord and Savior he also acknowledges his sins. In Matthew 3:6 and especially Mark 1:4-5, those whom John baptized confessed their sins in coming to the Messiah:

> John came baptizing in the wilderness and preaching a baptism of repentance for the remission of sins. And all the land of Judea, and those from Jerusalem, went out to him and were all baptized by him in the Jordan River, *confessing their sins.*

The point we made earlier is that faith implies repentance,

---

[51]One problem with this view of fellowship is that allegedly when the Christian sins, all sanctification stops. As R. B. Thieme wrongly says, we must "rebound" with 1 John 1:9 to get back in good with God and allow the process of sanctification to continue.

[52]See Calvin; F. F. Bruce on 1 John, p. 45; Canon A. E. Brooke in the ICC series on 1 John, p. 20; Lenski on 1 John, 392-94; Alford, 4:430.

the acknowledgement of our sins. Furthermore, Christians keep on confessing their sins until they enter heaven, ever acknowledging themselves as sinners and Jesus as their Lord and Savior. Someone may object that "confess" is in the present tense, indicating continual confession, thus for Christians only, not the initial confession of conversion. The present tense does not always mean continuous action, however, but often means customary, as here and in Mark 1 above. Thus when John includes himself in "we" confess our sins, he speaks of his justification and ongoing sanctification. Furthermore, comparing 1:4 with 2:1 and 1:8 with 2:4 indicates the "we" could be a literary plural, not to be taken literally.[53]

As Martin Luther so accurately said of 1 John 1:9:

> . . . this statement must be understood as referring to confession before God by which we ourselves confess our sins as well as our faith. Thus God finally forgives sin and grants grace and a pacified conscience by taking away the sting and the bits of conscience. . . . There it is a great gift of God to have His Word, to acknowledge sin on the basis of the Law, and to believe the Gospel. If one or the other is not true, God is charged with a lie and blasphemed.[54]

Therefore, "fellowship" in 1 John 1 means a relationship with God that necessarily includes communion, not an optional communion only. We have concluded this from the lexical definition of "fellowship," from its usage elsewhere in the New Testament, from other terms used around it in 1 John 1 such as light versus darkness, from John's usage of *in* and *of* and the present tense, and from the analogy of faith between Romans 3-4 with 1 John 1. As we continue to peruse 1 John, the absolute contrast between Christians and non-Christians is maintained.

---

[53]These grammars agree: F. Blass and A. DeBrunner, *A Greek Grammar of the New Testament and Other Early Christian Literature* (Chicago: The University of Chicago Press, 1970), #280; A. T. Robertson, *A Grammar of the Greek New Testament in the Light of Historical Research* (Nashville: Broadman Press, 1934), pp. 406, 678.

[54]Martin Luther, *Luther's Works: The Catholic Epistles* (St. Louis: Concordia Pub. House, 1967), pp. 231, 234.

Opposites in 1 John

In 1 John God's children are contrasted with the devil's children (3:4-10), the false teachers with the true (2:18-19; 4:1-6), the true believer with the professor (2:3-5; 3:10-15). Even as a son partakes of the physical characteristics of his earthly father, so those born again partake of the heavenly Father's moral nature: "If you know that He is righteous, you know that everyone who practices righteousness has been born of Him" (2:29). "Like father like son" is true in the spiritual realm also. It is not possible to be born *of God* and not be like Him.

When John says no murderer has eternal life abiding in him (3:15), the key word, according to Hodges, is *abiding*. One may *have* eternal life without having eternal life *abiding* in him.[55] With Dillow "eternal life" in this context means Jesus abiding in the believer, which in turn means the person is only out of fellowship with God when John says he does not have eternal life (p. 407). Now who is using theological interpretation and not observing the meanings of words? According to Dillow, eternal life means "final deliverance from hell" (Dillow's favorite expression) except when it has to do with perseverance; then it means optional fellowship and rewards. Incredible.

When John legislates that one's character reveals whether he belongs to Satan or Christ (3:10), what John meant, according to Dillow (p. 173), is that this is the way one can reveal his true spiritual father. In other words, if he chooses to live correctly, then it may be discerned by his character that his Father is God. But we should not conclude from this, Dillow and Hodges assert, that one's character is always meant to be a sure sign of his paternal relationship.[56] It can be if the Christian so chooses, but may not be if he chooses to live ungodly. The surest answer to such subterfuge is to quote the whole passage:

> Little children, let no one deceive you; the one who practices righteousness is righteous, just as He is righteous; the one who practices sin is of the devil; for the devil has sinned from the

---

[55]Hodges, *The Hungry Inherit*, p. 64.

[56]Hodges, p. 62.

beginning. The Son of God appeared for this purpose, that He might destroy the works of the devil. No one who is born of God practices sin, because His seed abides in him; and he cannot (practice) sin, because he is born of God. By this the children of God and the children of the devil are obvious: Anyone who does not practice righteousness is not of God, nor the one who does not love his brother (3:7-10).

Is not John clear? "*Anyone* who does not practice righteousness is not of God." John is saying that those born again partake of the nature of their Parent, God, and those not born again reveal their true parent, Satan. And why did God choose the figure "born again" except that it connotes that he partakes of the nature of his parents? Could any better figure have been chosen by God to communicate this Gospel truth? Of course not.

We know from the analogy of faith that John is not presenting sinless perfection because he says in 2:1-2 that Christians do sin. But he is telling us that sin cannot be master over the believer any more, for Christ came to destroy the devil's works, not to give believers the option to promote them.

We have analyzed 1 John to reach this conclusion: All these opposites in 1 John give us tests to discern the true Christian from the false, not the working Christian from the non-working one. One must believe Jesus is Messiah, God and man in one Person who died for his sins (1 John 4:1-6; 5:1). And if his faith is genuine, he will love righteousness (2:29), love the brethren (4:7-8), obey God (2:3-5) — in other words persevere. If he lacks these, according to 1 John, he must not conclude he is a Christian. Thus no Jehovah Witness, who denies the deity of Christ and His bodily resurrection, can have assurance, for he has not passed the objective test. Similarly, though one may be orthodox in doctrine, he cannot have assurance if he cannot pass the moral tests (2:3-5, 19, 29; 3:10; 4:7-8, 20). No amount of pumping himself up will give him the moral confirmations of his faith, for he must look to Jesus alone for these if he lacks them. The moral qualities are the fruits of a genuine faith, not the cause, and for one to pursue them directly is to chase after wind, to be a legalist. They are confirmations, effects of grace, so that the saint must by faith pursue the One who gives them, using the means of grace.

Conclusion

Beeke rightly says, "Happily, salvation's sureness does not rest on the believer's sureness of his salvation. . . ."[57] And how many of us, as a practical matter, judge the truth of a man's words by what he does more than by what he says? If a politician says he will not work for more taxes and then does so, do we not rightly regard him a hypocrite?[58] And is it not the case that Americans are being taught to disregard the personal life of a politician, for this allegedly does not affect his ability to serve the people, and that this very point is giving us the worst cadre of politicians in American history? Rather does not God say that if one cannot control his own house that he cannot be an elder (1 Tim. 3) in a church and that the same should apply to politicians?

In his book Beeke summarizes well the perseverance of the saints:

> The conclusion is clear: Despite backsliding and the great injury that ensues, God's people shall persevere. Their fruits shall "betray" them. Their perseverance is Trinitarian in its outworking and consists of (1) the perseverance of the Spirit within them; (2) the perseverance of Christ for them on Calvary and at the right hand of the Father; and (3) the perseverance of the Father's electing love of eternal good pleasure toward them.[59]

Therefore, the one who has assurance believes in the biblical Gospel, trusting in Jesus alone for forgiveness of sins (objective), and if his faith is genuine the Holy Spirit will sanctify him, convincing him that he is God's child, enabling him to love and practice God's commands (subjective).

---

[57]Beeke, *Assurance of Faith*, p. 143.

[58]In twentieth century America you can tell when a politician is lying by seeing if his lips are moving!

[59]Beeke, *Assurance of Faith*, p. 184.

6

Conclusion

Dillow's disparity hermeneutic, of interpreting the Bible in pitting one passage against another in lieu of reading passages in light of one another, leads him into serious trouble. He claims to hold to the semantic meanings of words, often denying their theological meanings, ignoring the analogy of faith. Thus he has faith versus works and not a faith that works; regeneration by faith instead of regeneration producing faith; John not having the word "repentance" means the idea is not present; faith void of repentance instead of faith that repents; works ("ought" or law) results in sanctification ("is" or grace) and not the reverse; and objective assurance versus subjective assurance when the Bible teaches that objective assurance leads to subjective assurance. At every point, I am convinced, it is Dillow's dispensational hermeneutic and Pelagian assumptions that lead him astray. Oozing distinctions and antinomianism from every pore, he oils his way through text after text. This hermeneutic has been the pride and joy of dispensationalists,[1] though more recent dispensational scholarship is moving away from the so-called "literal" interpretation.[2] The very fact that they are moving more toward a Reformed interpretation should tell the reader several things: After 150 years they are beginning to recognize their error of pitting one passage against another; they recognize how difficult it is to define "literal";[3] and they are

---

[1]Charles Ryrie, *Dispensationalism Today* (Chicago: Moody Press, 1969), p. 86ff.

[2]Edited by Craig A. Blaising and Darrell L. Bock, *Dispensationalism, Israel and the Church* (Grand Rapids: Zondervan, 1992), see especially the introduction.

[3]See my discussion of this in Curtis I. Crenshaw and Grover E. Gunn, *Dispensationalism Today, Yesterday, and Tomorrow* (Memphis: Footstool

recognizing that the Reformed have much to offer. Hopefully they will consistently work out this faulty hermeneutic until they arrive safely "home" in the Reformed camp.

Recall just a few of their departures from the historical interpretation that we have investigated: One who has dead faith (James 2) may still be a Christian because for faith to be dead it had to be alive once. Those who practice wickedness will not inherit the kingdom of God (Gal. 5:21; Eph. 5:5; 1 Cor. 6:9, 10), but this does not mean they will not go to heaven for "inheriting" the kingdom and "entering" the kingdom are not the same. When the Lord said you can tell the reprobate by their fruit (Matt. 7:20-23), He was not speaking of a change in their lives but what they said with their mouths. When John said that one's character revealed whether he was a child of Satan or of God (1 John 3:10ff), this does not mean that one is not a Christian if his life is not changed but only that he is living *like* Satan is his father. When John says that the one who is born of God does not practice sin (1 John 3:9), this refers to the Christian who is abiding in Christ, but not all Christians abide in Christ. John says that no murderer has eternal life abiding in him (1 John 3:15), but there is a difference between having eternal life and having it abide in him. Paul reveals that one who has been justified cannot continue in sin (Rom. 6:1), but this refers to what ought to happen, not to what does happen. Paul proclaims that the power of sin has been broken in the believer's life (Rom. 6:14), but this means only in position, not in practice. Peter (1 Peter 1:6-9), Hebrews (10:35-39), and James (James 1:21; 5:20) speak of persevering to the saving of the soul, but the "soul" in these verses only means the physical life. One who has to twist so many passages to make his theology fit obviously has hermeneutical problems.

Furthermore, Dillow's Pelagianism leads him to a faulty view of regeneration, making the Christian have two natures, and at his option he can choose to function through either one. This leaves the person virtually unchanged, the will unrenewed and supposedly neutral, having the innate moral ability to choose either sin or holiness. The new birth, according to him, is simply a new capacity instead of a new heart

Publications, 1985), Introduction.

that governs him. In the biblical view, all men are slaves, either to sin or holiness, but in Dillow's view, one can be neutral, suspended between the two, with man's "sovereign" will determining the outcome. But in Scripture one chooses according to his nature, his heart, his true self. In Dillow's understanding the will of the born again person is virtually untouched so that the Holy Spirit can only offer moral persuasion to do right but not effectual grace to guarantee results. Furthermore, in his view of sanctification the Spirit flows through the believer, leaving the Christian untouched with a substitutionary sanctification.

Dillow's faulty hermeneutic and distorted regeneration lead him even further awry with his denial that faith and repentance go together. His isolation hermeneutic causes him to conclude that because John speaks of faith to gain eternal life, that belief must be "self-evident," not including repentance or works. John must stand alone. When Paul says justification is by faith apart from works (Rom. 4:1ff), this allegedly means a faith devoid of works, for no other passage, such as James 2, can be considered. Romans 4 must stand alone. Since John does not mention the word "repentance" but only used faith, repentance allegedly must be excluded from justification. John must stand alone, and the idea of repentance cannot be considered as this would violate the semantic value of repentance. Since faith is most often the requirement for justification, it supposedly does not include repentance, for it usually stands alone.

According to Dillow, regeneration does not renew the will so the person is "free" to determine if he will have works or not. He may believe with the mind and not embrace Christ with the whole soul, for regeneration (Dillow teaches) is primarily something man does. If he does not choose to do good works, God will slap his wrist, but he will still "inherit" heaven, according to him.

Finally, as Dillow consistently works out his theology, if passages stand alone, if man is sovereign in his regeneration and regeneration does not renew the will and the whole person, if repentance and faith can exist apart from one another and apart from works, if justification and sanctification have no necessary connection, then assurance of faith is something man does and has nothing to do with fruit in one's life. If one says he is a Christian, then he is, for he knows whether his faith is real. The witness of the Spirit is irrelevant, for the professing Christian decides whether he is a child of God or not. Faith in one's faith or faith that one is not self-deceived is the all important matter. Fruit is unnecessary as confirmation, for the person — not God — determines if he will persevere. In regeneration, "like Father like son" is not relevant, as regeneration only adds another option.

The irony though is that the analogy of faith is used to determine what 1 John means so that 2:29 cannot mean that one's spiritual birth makes one like the Father, that 3:9 must refer to the believer's new nature that cannot sin, that a murderer who does not have eternal life (3:15) must mean that he is not enjoying his eternal life, and so forth.

The conclusion of the whole matter is that "there is nothing new under the sun." Dillow is another antinomian, semi-Pelagian in a line that stretches from Augustine who fought against Pelagius through the Reformers who fought against the Anabaptists and the Libertines. Some deny the Gospel by adding works as the condition for justification and others deny the Gospel by eliminating works as the necessary fruit of justification, the former being legalism and the latter license. Some of Dillow's arguments have a different twist, but the foundation on which he stands is the same as the others: the sovereign will of man, a "Christian" humanism, and resistible grace. His arguments have a sophisticated garb but once unclothed, they are the same old semi-Pelagianism, not a new solution between Arminianism and Calvinism. He has not sailed safely between the Scylla of legalism and the Charybdis of license; he has crashed against both. May the sovereign Triune God be pleased to deliver both him and his disciples. Amen.

> "Not everyone who says to Me, 'Lord, Lord,' shall *enter* [not inherit] the kingdom of heaven, but *he who does* the will of My Father in heaven. Many will say to Me in that day, 'Lord, Lord, have we not prophesied in Your name, cast out demons in Your name, and done many wonders in Your name?' And then I will declare to them, 'I never knew you; depart from Me, you who practice lawlessness!'" (Matt. 7:21-23).

Appendix 1

Handling Some Texts

Perhaps it would be profitable to consider a few more of Dillow's twistings in seeking to nullify the biblical doctrine of the perseverance of the saints. It has not been my purpose to handle every passage that Dillow distorts, for this would require a tome like his. Calvin was correct when he argued against the Libertines of his day, "For the only way to exterminate wicked sects and heresies is to yield to God's pure truth, which is the unique light that dispels darkness, as experience truly demonstrates."[1] The greatest defense against error is the truth. Also I have better things to do than spend weeks on something that the church has rejected for so many centuries and that is only a problem in a few circles. I have many pastoral duties that require much time. However, because Dillow and others who take the antinomian view pride themselves in proclaiming that only they state exactly what the Bible says while others engage in warping Scripture, we shall hopefully demonstrate to the candid reader that the Reformed actually do true exegesis.

John 15[2]

In this passage Jesus says regarding certain branches:

> Every branch in Me that does not bear fruit He takes away; and every [branch] that bears fruit He prunes, that it may bear more fruit. If anyone does not abide in Me, he is cast out as a

---

[1]John Calvin, *Treatises Against the Anabaptists and Against the Libertines* (Grand Rapids: Baker Book House, 1982), p. 210.

[2]For a detailed and good exegesis of this passage, read James E. Rosscup, *Abiding in Christ* (Grand Rapids: Zondervan Publishing House, 1973), especially chapters 15-17. I had done my research on John 15 about 17 years before reading Rosscup.

branch and is withered; and they gather them and throw [them] into the fire, and they[3] are burned (John 15:2, 6).

There have been extremes in understanding these verses, the Arminians believing that the branches lost their salvation while the license people say they lost their rewards. Of course, Dillow is in the latter group.

Dillow denies that the parallel passage in Isaiah 5 has anything to do with the Lord's statement, maintaining that the branches are true believers, that when the Lord says the branches are "taken away," this should be translated "lifted up," and that not people but their works are burned (p. 401ff).

First, Isaiah is indeed parallel to this passage, as the Lord rebukes His covenant people for their unfruitfulness and judges them. Though John does not quote the Old Testament directly very often, he is thoroughly saturated with its ideas and motifs, repeatedly using its imagery and parallels. Jesus, as the Lord incarnate, warns His disciples in the upper room that if they are not fruitful — like Judas who had just left to betray Him — like Israel of old, they would be judged. Dillow uses his dispensational hermeneutic to keep from seeing the parallel between Old Testament Israel and the church,[4] that God's covenant people may be in covenant with Him, as Judas was in the inner circle, and yet not be individually converted. Because of a faulty hermeneutic and because of the anti-covenantal assumption, Dillow misses the point of the passage. Of course Dillow uses the Old Testament to understand the New Testament's concept of inheritance, but his usage is "objective."

Secondly, that these "branches" are people and not fruit is seen by the context in which Judas has just been dismissed to do his betrayal. Furthermore, John says in verse 5, "I am the vine and *you* are the branches." He adds in verse 6: "If *anyone* does not abide in Me, *he* is cast out as a branch and is

---

[3]The verb "burned" is actually singular, but the subject is a neuter plural, which in the Greek idiom takes a singular verb. Therefore, the translation of "they" is correct.

[4]See the book written against dispensationalism by myself and Grover Gunn, entitled *Dispensationalism Today, Yesterday, and Tomorrow*, published by this same publisher. It can be ordered from the address at the front of this review book.

withered; and they gather them and throw [them] into the fire, and they are burned." The disciples are the branches, and if they do not abide in Him, the branches are cast into the fire and burned. This is obviously not their works. The "anyone" in verse 6 is a masculine pronoun (*tis*), and the "them" in "they gather *them*" refers grammatically back to the "branch."

The "casting out" is what Jesus said would never happen to those who were the true Israel, the true believers, using the same Greek words: "All that the Father gives Me will come to Me, and the one who comes to Me *I will by no means cast out*" (John 6:37). The branches broken off and burned, therefore, are covenant members who bear no fruit.

Dillow wants a different rendering for "takes away" (*airo*). He quotes R. K. Harrison to say that the word should be rendered "lifts up," as it allegedly is ten times in John. With this rendering the branches are not taken away but only lifted up for pruning, concluding that the branches are Christians who only need lifting up to bear fruit. Dillow does not document these ten places in John, and the only ones I could find had to do with "taking up" a bed (John 5:8ff) or "taking up" stones (John 8:59). The standard Greek lexicon agrees with the traditional rendering of "takes away."[5] The immediate context speaks of being "in Me," and its opposite would be "not in Me" or "taken away." The parallel in Isaiah 5 has a varied form of the word *airo* (*aphaipeo*) in which the rendering of the Hebrew and the Greek in the LXX is "take away." What more does one need? Notice the Isaiah context that Dillow summarily dismissed:

> What more could have been done to My vineyard that I have not done in it? Why then, when I expected it to bring forth [good] grapes, did it bring forth wild grapes? And now, please let Me tell you what I will do to My vineyard: *I will take away* its hedge, and it shall be burned; and break down its wall, and it shall be trampled down. I will lay it waste; it shall not be pruned or dug, but there shall come up briers and thorns. I will also command the clouds that they rain no rain on it. For the vineyard of the Lord of hosts is the house of Israel, and the

---

[5] Arndt and Gingrich, 2nd. ed., p. 24, 2nd edition.

men of Judah are His pleasant plant. He looked for justice, but behold, oppression; for righteousness, but behold, weeping (Isa. 5:4-7).

Consider Dillow's faulty exegesis. He disallows the Old Testament parallel to vine, ignores the flow of the context where the disciples are the branches, *assumes* that because a command is given to abide that it is optional, *assumes* that one cannot be in covenant with God and not regenerated, opts for a translation for "takes away" (*airo*) that is strained for this context, and ignores the following context where the Lord stated: "You did not choose Me, but I chose you and appointed you that you should go and bear fruit, and that *your fruit should remain*" (John 15:16). Also the Lord said: "Without Me you can no nothing" (John 15:5). Furthermore, "take away" is better horticulture, for a branch that is "withered" (v. 6) would not be lifted up but cut off. Then he has the audacity to state of the Reformed that they engage in "all kinds of fancy twistings and turnings" regarding this passage (p. 401).[6]

Also "abiding" in John is similar in meaning to other terms: "in the light," "in Him," "abiding in Him and He in you," "knowing God," and "born of God" (1 John 1:7-10; 2:8-11, 12-14, 3-6; 2:27-31, 6, 9-10; 4:7-8, 13-16; 5:1-5, 18-20). Furthermore we abide in Christ and He in us or neither occurs (1 John 2:23-24, 27; 3:6 with 9, 24; 4:13, 15-16). There is no partial abiding, where He is in us and we are not in Him. Even right here in John 15 we have mutual abiding (v. 5). Also, belief in Christ, loving God and man, and practicing righteousness are inseparable (1 John 2:3-5; 3:6-10, 14, 23; 4:20-21; 5:1-3, 18-20).

In John 6:54-56 those who "eat His flesh and drink His blood" have eternal life *and* abide in Him and He in them. To have Christ's "words abide in" one is equivalent to having eternal life (John 5:38-40). In the following chart, notice from 1 John how the terms in the top row are the same, and the terms in the first column are similar to one another and to the terms in the top row (unless otherwise stated all the

---

[6]For another excellent discussion of this passage see William Hendriksen's *New Testament Commentary: The Gospel of John*, p. 293ff.

references are from 1 John):

	In the light	In Him	Abiding in Him and He in us	Knowing God	Born of God
Practicing righteousness	1:6 with 7	2:5 with verses 3-4	2:6; 3:6, 9-10	2:3-4; 3:6	2:29; 3:9; 5:4, 18
Loving God and man	2:9-11	4:16	3:14-5, 17, 23-24; 4:12, 16	4:7	4:7
Belief in Jesus	1:7 with John 8:12; 12:35-36, 46	5:20	2:23-24; 3:23-24; 4:15	2:12 with v. 13	5:1
Opposite is spiritual death	1:6 with 7; John 3:19-21; 1:5; 8:12; 12:35, 46	2:4 with v. 5	3:14-15	2:3-4; 3:1, 6; 4:8	3:9-10; 4:7-8

One can peruse all these references and see how John loves to use slightly different terms to teach the same ideas. This is not simply a theological hermeneutic (though it is that), but the way John has actually done things.

Some may object that John says those to whom he is speaking are *cleansed* (John 15:3), which is to be justified (John 13:10), thus meaning that those about whom Jesus is speaking are only true believers. However, later on the Lord also says that they must abide or continue in Him or they would possibly be cast out, even as Paul recognized the same of himself in 1 Corinthians 9:27. They would not lose their salvation, but would indicate that they were never justified (1 John 2:19). We have covenantal language, as we saw earlier in the book, and those addressed can appear to be believers (see Chapter 1) and turn out to be unbelievers. Furthermore, it may be that Jesus' statement is meant only for the eleven, who were personally cleansed, while others are referred to as "anyone" (v. 6).

Another objection is that Jesus said "Every branch *in me* that does not bear fruit He takes away," so that the branches are "in Him." Again, this is covenantal language. It is unfortunate that our American individualism has removed us so far from the biblical covenants in which the many can represented by the one (Rom. 5:12ff), and also those in the covenant can be cast out, indicating that they were never personally regenerated. Scripture sometimes speaks of mankind as lost or justified, but it also speaks of mankind as in the covenant or not in the covenant. Those in the covenant may or may not be regenerated, but the strong language is used of all in the covenant. Furthermore, it is probable that "in Me" modifies the verb and not the noun, translated "every branch that does not bear fruit in Me," which would not indicate they are actually in Him.[7]

Saving the Soul

For you have need of endurance, so that after you have done the will of God, you may receive the promise: For yet a little while, and He who is coming will come and will not tarry. Now the just shall live by faith; but if anyone draws back, my soul has no pleasure in him. But we are not of those who draw back to perdition, but of those who believe to *the saving of the soul* (Heb. 10:36-39).

Therefore lay aside all filthiness and overflow of wickedness, and receive with meekness the implanted word, which is able *to save your souls* (James 1:21).

In this you greatly rejoice, though now for a little while, if need be, you have been grieved by various trials, that the genuineness of your faith, being much more precious than gold that perishes, though it is tested by fire, may be found to praise, honor, and glory at the revelation of Jesus Christ, whom having not seen you love. Though now you do not see [Him], yet believing, you rejoice with joy inexpressible and full of glory, receiving the end of your faith — *the salvation of [your] souls* (1 Peter 1:6-9).

One would think that there were no clearer words regarding the perseverance of the saints than these used of the

[7]Greek prepositional phrases usually modify verbs. Also John used "in Me" five other times in these verses (15:4 (twice), 5, 6, 7) and in each instance the phrase modifies the verb.

salvation of our souls. But Dillow, using his theological hermeneutic, argues from Matthew 16:24-26 that "saving the
soul" means to "save the physical life": "For what is a man
profited if he gains the whole world, and loses his own soul?
Or what will a man give in exchange for his soul?" Jesus does
not specifically say "save the soul," but Dillow's hermeneutic
is eclectic, seeking to find a meaning of "soul" that will
harmonize with his theology. Dillow says "soul" means physical life in this Matthew context. If true — and we doubt Dillow
is right — it would seem that in this context Jesus uses the
physical life to imply one's spiritual life as well. Furthermore,
Dillow *assumes* that the physical life and the spiritual life
cannot be intertwined, which is to fall into the gnostic trap·
that the physical and the spiritual are necessarily separate.
Such an idea is not biblical.[8] Usually in Scripture the physical
implies the spiritual and the reverse. Even if Dillow were right
about Matthew 16, would this nullify the other passages in the
New Testament on "saving the soul"? No.

Furthermore, Dillow says the Septuagint uses the expression "save the soul" eleven times and always means the
physical life. I have looked up his references, and he is not
correct. In Genesis 19:17 both Lot's life and soul are delivered
from Sodom, or would we say that the destruction of Sodom
had nothing to do with the residents' salvation? In Genesis
32:30 Jacob's "soul" is preserved when he sees the face of God,
which seems to be not only physical life but his salvation as
well. In 1 Kings 19:11 this would seem to be David's physical
life only. Judges 10:10-15 is no analogy to the New Testament,
for the only time "soul" is mentioned is of the Lord's "soul."
In Job 33:27-28, the saving seems to be of one's immaterial
soul: ". . . He has not punished me according to the full
amount of my sins. Save my soul, that it may not go to
destruction, and my life shall see the light." Psalm 30:7 refers
to the inner temporal life, not just the body (likewise Ps.
108:31). Psalm 71:13 refers to both physical and spiritual.
Jeremiah 31:6 is both. So much for Dillow's claim.

The point is that "save the soul" can refer to one's physical

---

[8]See Philip J. Lee, *Against The Protestant Gnostics* (New York: Oxford
University Press, 1987). A superb book for our day, and one will find
dispensational theology to be very gnostic.

life, to his spiritual life, or to both, the context determining which. Read again the contexts of the verses given above, and you will notice how far fetched Dillow's idea is. In Hebrews 10 they have "need of endurance" and must not draw back to "destruction," which term (*apoleian*) is often used of going to hell (Matt. 7:13; Rev. 17:8, 11; Phil. 1:28; 3:19; Rom. 9:22; 2 Peter 3:7, etc).[9] If they persevere, they will receive the *promise*, which in Hebrews is the Gospel (4:1ff, which they had preached to them but some did not believe), the new covenant (8:6), and the eternal inheritance (9:15) — not just rewards. Likewise, in other New Testament books the "promise" is Jesus, the Holy Spirit, and forgiveness of sins as foretold in the Old Testament (Acts 2:33-39; 13:32-39; 26:6ff; Rom. 1:2; 4:16; 15:8-9; Gal. 3 & 4; Eph. 2:11ff; 3:6ff, etc).

First Peter 1 says that the "genuineness of your faith" may be found to the praise of Christ when the readers endure various trials and that their faith will be so found "at the revelation of Jesus Christ." The latter expression seems to refer to His Second Coming, so is Peter referring to their physical lives? Were they going to live until the Second Coming? In verse 5 he says they "are kept by the power of God through faith for salvation ready to be revealed in the last time," and is this also just their physical lives? Is the "inheritance incorruptible and undefiled" also just the physical life? (Notice that the inheritance *is* the salvation.) Then Peter says in verse 9 that the end result of their faith is the "salvation of your souls," which in verse 10 is the "salvation the prophets have inquired and searched carefully, who prophesied of the grace that would come to you, searching what, or what manner of time, the Spirit of Christ was indicating when He testified beforehand of the sufferings of Christ and the glories that would follow." Obviously, to any unbiased reader who is not trying to justify a system, the "salvation of the soul" here is the eternal salvation of one's immortal soul.

---

[9]So Arndt and Gingrich agree, 2nd edition, p. 103, and list Hebrews 10:39 as an example.

Perseverance

Furthermore, on perseverance we read that we shall be partakers of this promise and of Jesus *if* "we hold the beginning of our confidence steadfast to the end" (Heb. 3:14) and we are Jesus' house "*if* we hold fast the confidence and the rejoicing of the hope firm to the end" (Heb. 3:6). Dillow seeks to circumnavigate the import of these last two verses by saying that this is sanctification and not justification, which has meaning only if the two are not inherently connected. On the contrary, it is both sanctification and justification, and Paul[10] argues from the effect (sanctification) to the cause (justification), warning that if they do not have sanctification that they do not have justification. In 2:14ff Paul speaks of Jesus as our propitiation and says that we can go to Him for help, which means that the justification is the umbrella for sanctification, that our justification leads us to Him for help in sanctification.

First John 2:19 could not be clearer: "They went out from us, but they were not of us; for *if they had been of us, they would have continued with us*; but [they went out] that they might be made manifest, that none of them were of us." Those who are true Christians continue with the fellowship. Dillow rightly says that "they" refers to the antichrists in the previous verse (p. 167), but this does not lessen the truth that if they had been genuine they would have persevered. Are only prophets required to persevere?

"Carnal" Christians in the New Testament

I shall give only a summary of these as the student is referred to the commentaries, most of which are Reformed,[11] for indepth answers to Dillow. It is also recommended that the student read the contexts around the disputed passages as these shed abundant light on Dillow's "exegesis."

---

[10]I believe Paul wrote Hebrews.

[11]It is noteworthy that most commentaries that even dispensationalists and Arminians use are done by the Reformed. It appears that they are not afraid of testing their theology by indepth exegesis of Scripture. Indeed, only the Reformed can sustain their theology by such a process.

The Corinthians are called "carnal" in 1 Corinthians 3, not because their whole lives were given over to disobedience, but because they were guilty of the sin of immaturity in identifying with leaders as if that were significant rather than identifying with God who caused the increase. On the positive side, they had broken with their sexual sins (1 Cor. 6:11) and were not lacking in any gift (1 Cor. 1:7).

Those who have some works burned up are teachers (1 Cor. 3:14, 15). These teachers have laid the good foundation of the Gospel (v. 11), but then have gone astray in some area. If this happens, they shall still be saved, but much of their effort shall be lost. Paul does not say that they have no fruit at all, for the foundation laid means salvation at least for themselves and their hearers.[12] This passage reminds me of James 3:1: "My brethren, let not many of you become teachers, knowing that we shall receive a stricter judgment."

Lot certainly sinned grievously in Sodom, but his "righteous soul was tormented from day to day by seeing and hearing their lawless deeds" (2 Peter 2:8). Peter continues that the Lord delivered him from temptation (v. 9), indicating that he was not given the option to live as he wanted.

Most of Dillow's other examples of so-called carnal Christians are lost people.

---

[12]This interpretation is shared by Calvin in his commentary, and Gordon Clark and F. W. Grosheide in their respective commentaries on 1 Corinthians.

Appendix Two

Warfield's Critique of Chafer

The following article by B. B. Warfield in 1918 is just one more indication of the problems in the anti-lordship movement, especially at DTS. The article is taken out of *Bibliotheca Sacra*, which journal was at Princeton when Dr. Warfield wrote but now, ironically, is at Dallas Theological Seminary. The article is a critique of the still popular book by Lewis Sperry Chafer (the primary founder of DTS who wrote a systematic theology), *He That Is Spiritual*. We turn now to the great prince of Princeton, B. B. Warfield. [All emphasis is his].

Mr. Chafer is in the unfortunate and, one would think, very uncomfortable, condition of having two inconsistent systems of religion struggling together in his mind. He was bred an Evangelical, and, as a minister of the Presbyterian Church, South, stands committed to Evangelicalism of the purest water. But he has been long associated in his work with a coterie of "Evangelists" and "Bible Teachers," among whom there flourishes that curious religious system (at once curiously pretentious and curiously shallow) which the Higher Life leaders of the middle of the last century brought into vogue; and he has not been immune to its infection. These two religious systems are quite incompatible. The one is the product of the Protestant Reformation and knows no determining power in the religious life but the grace of God; the other comes straight from the laboratory of John Wesley, and in all its forms — modifications and mitigations alike — remains incurably Arminian, subjecting all gracious workings of God to human determining. The two can unite as little as fire and water.[1]

---

[1] This is the same point I made in chapter 1, charging that the DTS brand of theology seeks to merge Pelagianism and Calvinism, resistible and irresistible grace.

Mr. Chafer makes use of all the jargon of the Higher Life teachers. In him, too, we hear of two kinds of Christians, whom he designates respectively "carnal men" and "spiritual men," on the basis of a misreading of 1 Corinthians 2:9ff (pp. 8, 109, 146); and we are told that the passage from the one to the other is at our option, whenever we care to "claim" the higher degree "by faith" (p. 146). With him, too, thus, the enjoyment of every blessing is suspended on our "claiming it" (p. 129). We hear here, too, of "letting" God (p. 84), and, indeed, we almost hear of "engaging" the Spirit (as we engage, say, a carpenter) to do work for us (p. 94); and we do explicitly hear of "making it possible for God" to do things (p. 148), — a quite terrible expression. Of course, we hear repeatedly of the duty and effi-cacy of "yielding" — and the act of "yielding ourselves" is quite in the customary manner discriminated from "consecrating" ourselves (p. 84), and we are told, as usual, that by it the gate is opened into the divinely appointed path (pp. 91, 49). The quie-tistic phrase, "not by trying but by a right adjustment," meets us (p. 39), and naturally such current terms as "known sin" (p. 62), "moment by moment triumph" (pp. 34, 60), "the life that is Christ" (p. 31), "unbroken walk in the Spirit" (pp. 53, 113), "unbroken victory" (p. 96), even Pearsall Smith's famous "at once": "the Christian may realize *at once* the heavenly virtues of Christ" (p. 39, the italics his). It is a matter of course after this that we are told that it is not *necessary* for Christians to sin (p. 125) — the emphasis repeatedly thrown on the word "neces-sary" leading us to wonder whether Mr. Chafer remembers that, according to the Confession of Faith to which, as a Presbyterian minister, he gives his adhesion, it is in the strictest sense of the term *not necessary* for anybody to sin, even for the "natural man" (ix, I).

Although he thus serves himself with their vocabulary, and therefore of course repeats the main substance of their teaching, there are lengths, nevertheless, to which Mr. Chafer will not go with his Higher Life friends. He quite decidedly repels, for example, the expectation of repetitions of the "Pentecostal manifestations" (p.47), and this is the more notable because in his expositions of certain passages in which the charismatic Spirit is spoken of he has missed that fact, to the confusion of his doctrine of the Spirit's modes of action. With equal decisiveness

he repels "such man-made, unbiblical terms as 'second blessing', 'a second work of grace', 'the higher life', and various
phrases used in the perverted statements of the doctrines of
sanctification and perfection" (pp. 31, 33), including such
phrases as "entire sanctification" and "sinless perfection" (pp.
107, 139). He is hewing here, however, to a rather narrow line,
for he does teach that there are two kinds of Christians, the
"carnal" and the "spiritual"; and he does teach that it is quite
unnecessary for spiritual men to sin and that the way is fully open
to them to live a life of unbroken victory if they choose to do so.

Mr. Chafer opens his book with an exposition of the closing
verses of the second and the opening verses of the third chapters
of 1 Corinthians. Here he finds three classes of men contrasted,
the "natural" or unregenerate man, and the "carnal" and "spiritual" men, both of whom are regenerated, but the latter of whom
lives on a higher plane. "There are two great spiritual changes
which are possible to human experience," he writes (p.8), —
"the change from the 'natural' man to the saved man, and the
change from the 'carnal' man to the 'spiritual' man. The former
is divinely accomplished when there is real faith in Christ; the
latter is accomplished when there is a real adjustment to the
Spirit. The 'spiritual' man is the divine ideal in life and ministry,
in power with God and man, in unbroken fellowship and blessing." This teaching is indistinguishable from what is ordinarily
understood by the doctrine of a "second blessing," "a second
work of grace," "the higher life." The subsequent expositions
only make the matter clearer. In them the changes are rung on
the double salvation, on the one hand from the *penalty* of sin, on
the other from the *power* of sin — "salvation into safety" and
"salvation into sanctity" (p. 109). And the book closes with a
long-drawn-out analogy between these two salvations. This
"analogy" is announced with this statement: "The Bible treats
our deliverance from the bond servitude to sin as a distinct form
of salvation and there is an analogy between this and the more
familiar aspect of salvation which is from the guilt and penalty
of sin" (p. 141). It ends with this fuller summary: "There are a
multitude of sinners for whom Christ has died who are not now
saved. On the divine side everything has been provided, and they
have only to enter by faith into His saving grace as it is for them
in Christ Jesus. Just so, there are a multitude of saints whose sin

nature has been perfectly judged and every provision made on the divine side for a life of victory and glory to God who are not now realizing a life of victory. They have only to enter by faith into the saving grace from the power and dominion of sin. . . . Sinners are not saved until they trust the Savior, and saints are not victorious until they trust the Deliverer. God has made this *possible* through the cross of His Son. Salvation from the power of sin must be claimed by faith" (p. 146). No doubt what we are first led to say of this is the quintessence of Arminianism. God saves no one — He only makes salvation *possible* for men. Whether it becomes *actual* or not depends absolutely on their act. It is only by their act that it is made *possible* for God to save them. But it is equally true that here is the quintessence of the Higher Life teaching, which merely emphasizes that part of this Arminian scheme which refers to the specific matter of sanctification. "What He provides and bestows is in the fullest divine perfection; but our adjustment is human and therefore subject to constant improvement. The *fact* of our possible deliverance, which depends on Him alone, does not change. We will have as much at any time as we make it possible for Him to bestow" (p. 148).

When Mr. Chafer repels the doctrine of "sinless perfection" he means, first of all, that our sinful natures are not eradicated. Entering the old controversy waged among perfectionists between the "Eradicationists" and "Suppressionists," he ranges himself with the latter — only preferring to use the word "control." "The divine method of dealing with the sin nature in the believer is by direct and unceasing *control* over that nature by the indwelling Spirit" (p. 134). One would think that this would yield at least a sinlessness of conduct; but that is to forget that, after all, in this scheme the divine action waits on man's. "The Bible teaches that, while the divine provision is one of *perfection* of life, the human appropriation is always *faulty* and therefore the results are *imperfect* at best" (p. 157). God's provisions only make it *possible* for us to live without sinning. The result is therefore only that we are under no *necessity* of sinning. But whether we shall sin or not is our own affair. "His provisions are always *perfect*, but our appropriation is always *imperfect*." "What He provides and bestows is in the fullest divine perfection, but our adjustment is human. . . . The fact of our possible deliverance, which depends on Him alone, does not change. We will have as much at any time as we make it possible for Him to *bestow*" (pp. 148, 149). Thus it comes about that we can be told that "the child of God and citizen of heaven may live a superhuman life, in harmony with his heavenly calling by an unbroken walk in the Spirit" — that "the Christian may realize *at once* the heavenly virtues of Christ" (p. 39); and that, in point of fact, he does nothing of the kind, that "all Christians *do* sin" (p. 111). A possibility of not sinning which is unillustrated by a single example and will never be illustrated by a single example is, of course, a mere postulate extorted by a theory. It is without practical significance. A universal effect is not accounted for by its possibility.

Mr. Chafer conducts his discussion of these "two general theories as to the divine method of dealing with the sin nature in believers" on the presumption that "both theories cannot be true, for they are contradictory" (p. 135). "The two theories are irreconcilable," he says (p. 139). "We are either to be delivered by the abrupt removal of all tendency to sin, and so no longer need the enabling power of God to combat the power of sin, or we are to be delivered by the immediate and constant power of the indwelling Spirit." This irreducible "either/or" is unjustified. In point of fact, both "eradication" and "control" are true. God delivers us from our sinful nature, not indeed by "abruptly" but by progressively eradicating it, and meanwhile controlling it. For the new nature which God gives us is not an absolutely new somewhat, alien to our personality, inserted into us, but our old nature itself remade — a veritable recreation, or making of all things new. Mr. Chafer is quite wrong when he says: "Salvation is not a so-called 'change of heart.' It is not a transformation of the old: it is a regeneration, or creation, of something wholly new, which is possessed in conjunction with the old so long as we are in the body" (p. 113). That this furnishes out each Christian with two conflicting natures does not appall him. He says, quite calmly: "The unregenerate have but one nature, while the regenerate have two" (p. 116). He does not seem to see that thus the man is not saved at all: a different, newly created, man is substituted for him. When the old man is got rid of — and that the old man has to be ultimately got rid of he does not doubt — the saved man that is left is not at all the old man that was to be saved, but a new man that has never needed any saving.

It is a temptation to a *virtuoso* in the interpretation of Scripture to show his mettle on hard places and in startling places. Mr. Chafer has not been superior to this temptation. Take but one example. "All Christian love," he tells us (p. 40) "according to the Scriptures, is distinctly a manifestation of divine love *through* the human heart" — a quite unjustified assertion. But Mr. Chafer is ready with an illustration. "A statement of this is found," he declares, "at Romans 5:5, 'because the love of God is shed abroad (lit., gushes forth) in our hearts by (produced, or caused by) the Holy Spirit, which is given unto us.' " Then he comments as follows: "This is not the working of human affection; it is rather the direct manifestation of the 'love of God' passing *through* the heart of the believer *out from* the indwelling Spirit. It is the realization of the last petition of the High Priestly prayer of our Lord: 'That the love wherewith thou hast loved me may be in them' (John 17:26). It is simply God's love working *in* and *through* the believer. It could not be humanly produced, or even imitated, and it of necessity goes out to the objects of divine affection and grace, rather than to the objects of human desire. A human heart cannot *produce* divine love, but it can *experience* it. To have a heart that feels the compassion of God is to drink of the wine of heaven." All this *bizarre* doctrine of the transference of God's love, in the sense of His active power of loving, to us, so that it works out from us again as new centres, is extracted from Paul's simple statement that by the Holy Spirit which God has given us His love to us is made richly real to our apprehension! Among the parenthetical philological comments which Mr. Chafer has inserted into his quotation of the text, it is a pity that he did not include one noting that "*ekcheo*" is not "*eischeo*," and that Paul would no doubt have used "*eischeo*" had he meant to convey that idea.

A haunting ambiguity is thrust upon Mr. Chafer's whole teaching by his hospitable entertainment of contradictory systems of thought. There is a passage near the beginning of his book, not well expressed it is true, but thoroughly sound in its fundamental conception, in which expression is given to a primary principle of the Evangelical system, which, had validity been given to it, would have preserved Mr. Chafer from his regrettable dalliance with the Higher Life formulas. "In the

Bible," he writes, "the divine offer and condition for the cure of sin in an unsaved person is crystallized into the one word 'believe'; for the forgiveness of sin with the unsaved is only offered as an indivisible part of the whole divine work of salvation. The saving work of God includes many mighty undertakings other than the forgiveness of sin, and salvation depends only upon *believing*. It is not possible to separate some one issue from the whole work of His saving grace, such as forgiveness, and claim this apart from the indivisible whole. It is, therefore, a grevious error to direct an unsaved person to seek forgiveness of his sins as a separate issue. A sinner minus his sins would not be a Christian; for salvation is more than subtraction, it is addition. 'I give unto them eternal life.' Thus the sin question with the unsaved will be cured as a part of, but never separate from, the whole divine work of salvation, and this salvation depends upon *believing*" (p. 62).[2] If this passage means anything, it means that salvation is a unit, and that he who is invited to Jesus Christ by faith receives in Him not only justification — salvation from the *penalty* of sin — but also sanctification — salvation from the *power* of sin — both "safety" and "sanctity." These things cannot be separated, and it is a grievous error to teach that a true believer in Christ can stop short in "carnality," and, though having the Spirit *with* him and *in* him, not have Him *upon* him — to use a not very lucid play upon prepositions in which Mr. Chafer indulges. In his attempt to teach this, Mr. Chafer is betrayed (p. 29) into drawing out a long list of characteristics of the two classes of Christians, in which he assigns to the lower class practically all the marks of the unregenerate man. Salvation is a process; as Mr. Chafer loyally teaches, the flesh continues in the regenerate man and strives against the Spirit — he is to be commended for preserving even to the Seventh Chapter of Romans its true reference — but the remainders of the flesh in the Christian do not constitute his characteristic. He is in the Spirit and is walking, with however halting steps, by the Spirit; and it is to all Christians, not to some, that the great promise is

---

[2]Chafer held to the unity of salvation, but, like Dillow, Hodges, Ryrie, and Zuck, his semi-Pelagianism made him schizophrenic, also espousing a second and optional work of grace called sanctification. As I have stated all through the book, contradictions are not new to Chafer and his legacy, for they have never understood Pelagianism and never extricated themselves from some form of it.

given, "Sin shall not have dominion over you," and the great assurance is added, "Because ye are not under the law but under grace." He who believes in Jesus Christ is under grace, and his whole course, in its process and in its issue alike, is determined by grace, and therefore, having been predestined to be conformed to the image of God's Son, he is surely being conformed to that image, God Himself seeing to it that he is not only called and justified but also glorified. You may find Christians at every stage of this process, for it is a process through which all must pass; but you will find none who will not in God's own good time and way pass through every stage of it. There are not two kinds of Christians, although there are Christians at every conceivable stage of advancement towards the one goal to which all are bound and at which all shall arrive.

Appendix 3

Antinomianism in Dispensationalism

Antinomianism has many facets,[1] but we shall consider that which is inherent in antinomianism: a denial that works have any *necessary* place in salvation. Antinomianism can appear anywhere. It appears in some Primitive Baptists who believe in "time salvation," that those regenerated may not have faith and works at all. This is hyper-Calvinism at its worst. Then the Libertines in Calvin's day were pantheistic, believing that since we are a part of "God" that what we do by definition is right. There is no place for the law of God for those who are "God." The Christian Scientists of today are analogous. Coming to the American continent, we find the Quakers and Ann Hutchinson, the former denying the Bible altogether and seeking for "God" within so that *they* decided what was right, not some external Bible. Hutchinson denied that sanctification had any *necessary* part in salvation and maintained that personal assurance was achieved by direct revelation from God within. If anyone doubted — for any reason — he was obviously not a Christian. John Cotton and others excommunicated her while she pronounced anathemas on him and the other ministers, saying God had revealed to her what would come upon them, but her "prophecies" never came true. She was killed by the Indians not long afterwards. But antinomianism especially appears in dispensationalism. Why?

[1] See *The New Schaff-Herzog Encyclopedia of Religious Knowledge* (Grand Rapids: Baker Book House, 1977), 1:196ff; Cotton Mather, *The Great Works of Christ in America* (Edinburgh: The Banner of Truth Trust, 1702, 1979), 2:508ff; Edwin H. Palmer, *The Encyclopedia of Christianity* (Wilmington: National Foundation for Christian Foundation, 1964), 1:270ff; John Calvin, *Treatises Against the Anabaptists and the Against the Libertines* (Grand Rapids: Baker Book House, 1982), p. 159ff.

Historically, the founder of DTS, Lewis Sperry Chafer, studied at Oberlin, the school founded by the virtually pure Pelagians, Asa Mahan and Charles Finney. Chafer had no formal theological training, being a musician. And though he did not pursue theology at Oberlin, the Pelagian assumption of human autonomy was undoubtedly absorbed by Chafer from the school. One who is not aware of this assumption tends to develop his theology around it, controlling every doctrine he believes. Indeed, in a sense there is no heresy except Pelagianism, for every false doctrine can be traced to it. There is not a cult in existence that denies "free will," with the possible exception of Islam, though if they really received the revelation of God through Scripture instead of trying to manufacture their own based on human sovereignty, they would be orthodox. I have read all seven volumes of Chafer's theology, and he did not understand Pelagianism. This confusion continues in his legacy, especially among those directly influenced by him, saying that in the converted there will be some change, somehow, but man is in charge.[2]

The root of all legalistic and license heresies is Pelagianism, the idea that man is good, that man has the ability to please God either without His grace or by using His grace at man's initiative. It is this latter concept that is especially prominent at DTS: that God is always waiting for the sinner to do something so that one uses God's grace for his own benefit. Unfortunately, DTS has infected much of the evangelical world in America with this errant teaching. This semi-Pelagianism is both legalistic and given to license.

It is legal in that God is seen as always waiting to grant the sinner some favor, thus the only hindrance is the will of man. All man has to do is. . . . The answer varies with the form of antinomianism involved, but at DTS and in dispensationalism in general the answer is faith so that faith obligates God and becomes a work; hence legalism. This sovereignty of man is carried over into the whole of salvation so that once one has *allowed* God to justify him, he can allow or disallow God to sanctify him; hence license. Just as justification was up to man, so sanctification is too. The irony is that what are seemingly

---

[2]Charles Ryrie, *So Great Salvation* (Victor Books, 1989), pp. 46-47; Roy Zuck, *Kindred Spirit*, published by DTS, Summer 1989, p. 5.

opposites, legalism and antinomianism, actually are Siamese twins, born of the same hideous parents, the old idol "free will" and human goodness. That man is seen to be good is obvious in that any time he chooses he can improve the grace already *available* to him and get himself saved. Others who had the same opportunity did not improve their grace, making the difference in the sinner, not in God's grace. In other words, if each sinner has equal opportunity to avail himself of God's grace, the one who does is better than the one who does not. To the degree that man is able to please God, to that degree he is good, whether the goodness extends to his whole being with him earning his "salvation" by works (Pelagianism) or extends partially with him earning it by faith (semi-Pelagianism).

Some dispensationalists, like John MacArthur and the Master's seminary, reject semi-Pelagianism, and for this we are grateful. But there is still an antinomianism inherent in dispensationalism, waiting to manifest itself. Why do dispensationalists tend to reject works of any kind as necessary in salvation, even as the fruit? There are theological reasons inherent in dispensationalism that give the answer: They (1) place a wall between law and grace, (2) deny that Old Testament saints were justified by faith in Jesus, (3) maintain that Jesus is not ruling now, and (4) assert that the Old Testament biblical covenants were only unconditional. These four seemingly unrelated beliefs are actually related, all in some way disconnecting good works as the *necessary* product of grace.

Law versus Grace

This should not be law *versus* grace but law and grace implying one another, but dispensationalists think that law and grace are not connected. The Old Testament was supposedly a time of law and the New Testament a time of grace, which places a wall between law and grace. Even though the neo-dispensationalists place both law and grace in each time period, there is still a mental wall between the concepts. They do not see that the law is about righteousness and the Gospel is about righteousness, implying one another, as Paul teaches in Romans 3:20ff; 6:14; Galatians 3:24, and so on. The law demands righteousness and the Gospel gives it, enabling us by the Spirit to produce holiness or the righteousness of the law in our lives (Rom. 3:31; 8:4). But according to dispensationalism, one need not turn from sin (law) to be justified (grace), for law and grace have nothing to do with one another. If one need not turn from his sins to be justified, he has made the law irrelevant, which carries over into sanctification, making obedience optional. The wall between law and grace is also between justification (grace) and sanctification (law).

Craig A. Blaising, a current professor of systematic at DTS, has noted the truth that "Chafer's dualistic synthesis wove his doctrine of . . . sanctification . . . with a problematic law-grace result."[3] Blaising thinks that he and others are overcoming this problem, but until they can see that law and grace imply one another and that salvation is the same in both Testaments, they will continue to be antinomian.

Daniel P. Fuller is very astute in his analysis of dispensationalism and of the relationship between law and grace, but he does not understand the Reformed position, which he castigates for having a law-grace dichotomy.[4] The Reformed have a dichotomy, but it is not absolute as the dispensationalists, believing rather that the connection between law and grace is righteousness: the Gospel is about righteousness, and the law is righteous. The law is God's commandments and shows us what God requires but is unable to produce the requisite righteousness; the Gospel gives legal righteousness in justification as a free gift, and consequently sanctifying righteousness is produced in us by the Spirit, enabling us to perform the law, though not perfectly in this life. Thus law and grace are connected by righteousness. The law leads to the Gospel, and then the Gospel in turn back to the law. The law reveals God's righteousness (1 Peter 1:13-16), and the Gospel gives it to the believer. The Reformed do not believe that keeping the law brings sanctification but that sanctification enables the believer to keep the law. Because dispensationalism separates the two absolutely, one can have grace

---

[3]Craig A. Blaising, *Dispensationalism, Israel and the Church* (Grand Rapids: Zondervan Publishing House, 1992), p. 223.

[4]See the extended discussion of these things in Daniel P. Fuller, *Gospel & Law: Contrast or Continuum?* (Grand Rapids: Wm. B. Eerdmans Pub. Co., 1980).

without law-keeping. As Berkhof says in refutation of Fuller's understanding of the Reformed:

> The law seeks to awaken in the heart of man contrition on account of sin, while the gospel aims at the awakening of saving faith in Jesus Christ. The work of the law is in a sense preparatory to that of the gospel. It deepens the consciousness of sin and thus makes the sinner aware of the need of redemption. *Both are subservient to the same end*, and both are indispensable parts of the means of grace. This truth has not always been sufficiently recognized. The condemning aspect of the law has sometimes been stressed at the expense of its character as a part of the means of grace. Ever since the days of Marcion there have always been some who saw only contrast between law and the gospel and proceeded on the assumption that the one excluded the other. . . . They lost sight of the fact that Paul also says that the law served as a tutor to lead men to Christ (Gal. 3:24), and that the Epistle to the Hebrews represents the law, not as standing in antithetical relation to the gospel, but rather as the gospel in its preliminary and imperfect state [emphasis added].[5]

The law leads us to Christ, and Christ leads us to the law. One cannot have the righteousness of Christ and reject the righteousness of the law. Christ in His life was obedient to the law and this obedience is imputed to us.[6] In being conformed to the moral image of Christ, believers are being made holy, like the law. Perfect holiness entails perfect law-keeping. The law is not a legal requirement to merit salvation or the power for sanctification but the path over which sanctification leads us.

Also dispensationalists deny the active obedience of

---

[5]Berkhof, *Systematic Theology*, p. 612.

[6]See Hebrews 2:10 ("in bringing many sons to glory, to make the author of their salvation perfect through sufferings") where the participle "bringing" is simultaneous with "to perfect" so that as Christ was being perfected He was at the same time bringing many sons to glory. In other words, as He obeyed, He was bringing. See A. A. Hodge, *The Atonement*, p. 253. His being perfected was counting for the "many sons." The perfecting was not His being made personally righteous as though the sinless Son of God had personal sin, but the completion of a life of perfect obedience. His perfect obedience to the law is imputed to us, not His attribute of righteousness. Christ obeyed for His people as He owed no obedience to the law for Himself. See also Romans 5:12ff; Philippians 2:7-8.

Christ, saying that only what He did on the Cross was vicarious and atoning.[7] Consistent with this, they say that when one is justified he only receives cancellation of guilt and judgment and not the active obedience of Christ in His stead, which leads them to the conclusion that the Christian need not obey the law since this is not an issue in Christ's work. Again there is an absolute dichotomy between law and grace, and just as Jesus did not have to satisfy the positive demands of the law for His people, neither do we.

If the moral laws of the Old Testament are not for today, as dispensationalists say, then we have a dichotomy between the moral precepts for Israel and the precepts for the church. This means that God's laws are not unified, that God has one moral code for one period of time and another code for a different period, which implies that God's laws are arbitrary. If they are arbitrary, God having changed His mind about moral law for today as opposed to the Old Testament, then all morality would seem to be legitimate (or illegitimate). This would also imply that there can be many lawgivers or gods, each with his own sphere of authority. Thus there is one way of salvation and moral code for Israel and another for the church. This dichotomy further implies that God's truth is not one, that "truths" can exist in isolation from one another, which would imply that God is not one. *It cannot be stated too strongly that seeing parts of the Bible as isolated from one another is a major, inherent weakness of dispensationalism*, implying all that we have just stated.

Rather, every part of the Bible necessarily infers the rest. God's Word is like white light that can be analyzed with a prism into its various hues but is always one. For the dispensationalists to think they have stated something significant when they criticize the Reformed of reading the New Testament back into the Old is to confirm our indictment. To interpret passages independently of the rest of the Bible implies two (or more) ways of salvation, gods, peoples, moral

[7]We recognize that the Lord's whole life of obedience was both active and passive, but the emphasis of His work on the Cross was passive. For validation of the typical dispensational view on this, see Robert P. Lightner, professor of systematic theology at DTS, *The Death Christ Died* (Des Plaines, IL: Regular Baptist Press, 1967), p. 19ff.

codes for the path of sanctification, and is gnostic to the core. We are not surprised, therefore, to see Normal Geisler say that

> Premillenarians do not believe the millennium will come about by any political process continuous with the present. They insist rather on a divine, cataclysmic, and supernatural inauguration of the reign of Christ on earth. This relieves premillennialists of any divine duty to Christianize the world. Their duty is to be salt, light, and to do good to all men. . . . They can be content with a democracy or any government which allows freedom to preach the gospel. . . . And their obligation is to promote a good and just government (1 Tim. 2:1-4), *not necessarily a uniquely Christian one.*[8]

Premillenarians need not work for Christian civil laws but only for fair ones.

The Ten Commandments are a case in point. Postmillennial theonomy, and its stepchild biblionomy, demands that the Ten Commandments are the basis for civil law. This, however, is impossible if *true freedom* of religion is to be allowed. For the first commandment(s) demands allegiance to a monotheistic God as opposed to all false gods or idols. If the civil law of the United States followed the Ten Commandments, *then there would be no freedom of religion for polytheists, Taoists, Hindus, Buddhists, secular humanists, or atheists. So making the Bible the basis for civil law is a contradiction to freedom of religion such as exists in the United States today. But if the Bible is not the basis for civil law, then what is?*

But nowhere in the Bible is God's judgment of the nations based on His special written revelation (the Bible). Rather it is always based on general principles of goodness and justice known to all men by general revelation (cf. Amos 1; Obad. 1; Jonah 3:8-10; Nahum 2) [emphasis added].[9]

---

[8]If one can define "good" apart from God, then we have gnosticism, the separation of things into two independent parts, not implying one another.

[9]*Bibliotheca Sacra*, third quarter, 1985, pp. 256-257, 261. See Leviticus 18, 20, and the first thirty or so chapters of Isaiah to confirm that God did indeed indict and judge nations for violations of His law. Did God judge Sodom and Gomorrah for violation of some law code that man had invented?

If God's nature and character do not change, how could His moral code and salvation change?

Old Testament Salvation versus New Testament Salvation

We should not say Old Testament salvation *versus* New Testament salvation but that the two are the same. But dispensationalists do not see salvation as the same for both testaments. Dallas Theological Seminary's doctrinal statement reads: "We believe that it was historically impossible that they [Old Testament saints] should have had as the conscious object of their faith the incarnate, crucified Son, the Lamb of God." The doctrinal statement goes on to explain that the Old Testament saints did not understand the types and sacrifices and that their faith was manifested in other ways, making reference to Hebrews 11 as proof of this. Thus Abraham was justified because he believed he would have numerous seed, making the content of his faith having nothing to do with his sin and repentance, even though Scripture indicates the opposite when he offered up Isaac and Jesus said he rejoiced to see His day (John 8:56). Likewise many of the other Old Testament saints. That this is a false view should be obvious (John 1:41, 46; 3:3-4, 10; 4:25; 5:39; 8:56; Luke 2:25-26, 38; 24:25-27, 44-47; Acts 10:43; Rom. 1:1-3; 4:1-4; 9:33; Gal. 3:8-10, 26, 29; 1 Cor. 10:2-4; Eph. 2:12; Heb. 11:24-26; 1 Peter 1:11; Ps. 2; Job 16:19; 19:25, etc.).[10]

Dispensationalists are constantly changing, but Lewis Sperry Chafer held that Israel was earthly and the church heavenly, that Israel was saved by her works and the church

---

[10]See the book Grover Gunn and I wrote against dispensationalism, *Dispensationalism Today, Yesterday, and Tomorrow*, where I take quite a few pages to show that the Old Testament saints indeed had faith in the coming Messiah. Though their faith was not as developed as ours, there still was a core truth of Messiah and His death and resurrection for their sins. How else could we explain Isaiah 53, Hebrews 11:26, 40, etc? If one tries to use the New Testament to understand the Old Testament saints' faith, dispensationalists respond that we are reading the New Testament back into the Old, to which we say, so what? Again their disparity hermeneutic leads them astray in pitting one passage (New Testament) against another (Old Testament).

by Christ.[11] Keeping with this defective view of Old Testament faith, they have Old Testament Israel married to Yahweh and the New Testament church married to Christ, making God a bigamist. The newer dispensationalists say that Israel and the church will eventually be merged, but nevertheless they are two separate entities until some time in eternity. But this dualism displays itself all through their theology: two peoples of God, two ways of salvation, law versus grace, earthly versus heavenly, two comings of Christ (rapture and Second Coming), which concludes in justification versus sanctification and faith versus works.

Dispensationalists despise the charge of two ways of salvation (union with Christ, regeneration, justification, sanctification, glorification), but when they still maintain that Old Testament saints had a different content to faith than New Testament saints, eliminating sin and Jesus, that they either were not regenerated or were not permanently indwelt by the Holy Spirit, this is two ways. The Reformed maintain that the content always has had a common kernel but expanded as time went on, while they say the content was completely different.

Dispensationalists find themselves on the horns of a very sharp dilemma: If the Old Testament saints were saved in the same way as New Testament ones, then they were regenerated, believed in the coming Messiah, had the Holy Spirit permanently, are in union with Christ as their Head, and do works by God's grace so that we must ask what possible difference could there be between Israel and the church? But if the Old Testament saints were not regenerated, did not believe in Jesus, did not have the Holy Spirit, or were not in union with Christ, then we necessarily have different ways of salvation.

Furthermore, there is no salvation without union with Jesus, which makes one a member of the church universal, and if one is in union with Jesus, then even if he is Moses he is in the church (Eph. 1:4ff; 2:11ff; Rom. 5:12-21; 1 Cor. 15:22ff). Indeed, the church is Israel (Gal. 6:16; Matt. 18:17;

---

[11]Chafer stated in his theology: "Men [in the Old Testament] were therefore just because of their own works for God, whereas New Testament justification is God's work for man in answer to faith." *Systematic Theology*, 7:219.

1 Peter 2:9-10; Rev. 21:12) and Israel is the church (Acts 7:38; Eph. 2:11ff, etc). The Bible can make this identification because there are not two ways of salvation and because Christ is the Head of the *one* elect people. If we are saved the same way, there are not two peoples of God; if there are two peoples of God, we must not be saved the same way. Thus by their dichotomy between Israel and the church and between law and Gospel, dispensationalists fall into legalism in the Old Testament and license in the New, for Israel had primarily law and had to help save herself while the church has primarily grace and needs no obedience.

Also dispensationalists deny that the Old Testament saints were permanently indwelt by the Holy Spirit or were born again or both. In John 3, however, the Lord marvels that Nicodemus is a teacher of Israel and does not understand the new birth, indicating that it was not something new. Furthermore, if the Old Testament saints did not live a godly life by the power of the Holy Spirit because they were supposedly not indwelt, then we have pure Pelagianism, living by one's own ability. Or if they were not born again, we have the worst possible heresy of a salvation by human works, which again would be pure Pelagianism.

As a side comment, I should observe that dispensationalists say Old Testament saints were not permanently indwelt by the Holy Spirit.[12] If this is so, then how did they live a life for God, by raw will power? If this is their answer, then we have pure Pelagianism, the doctrine of pleasing God by human effort. They sometimes argue their case from John 14:17, the Spirit "abides *with* you and will be *in* you." They draw the conclusion from the prepositions and the future tense that the Spirit was not *in* the twelve disciples then — only *with* them. The Spirit would be *in* them sometime in the future. Since the twelve were still "under law," they draw the further conclusion that no Old Testament saint was permanently indwelt by the Holy Spirit.

The statement by David in Psalm 51:11 where he prayed that God would not take His Spirit from him is covenantal,

---

[12]The "moderate" dispensationalists still hold that Old Testament saints were not permanently indwelt: Craig A. Blaising, *Dispensationalism, Israel and the Church* (Grand Rapids: Zondervan Publishing House, 1992), p. 78ff, 82, 86ff.

revealing that David feared for his salvation.[13] If God's Spirit were taken from him, it would indicate that he had never truly been regenerated (see 1 John 2:19). This is what happened to Saul in 1 Samuel 16:14 when the Spirit left him, and an evil spirit came on him. Perseverance of the saints is an Old Testament doctrine as well as a New Testament one. Thus asking for the Holy Spirit is asking for persevering grace (Luke 11:13). We see the Holy Spirit removed from those who had not persevered in the covenant in Hebrews 6:4-6:

> For it is impossible for those who were once enlightened, and have tasted the heavenly gift, and have become partakers of the Holy Spirit, and have tasted the good word of God and the powers of the age to come, if they fall away, to renew them again to repentance, since they crucify again for themselves the Son of God, and put [Him] to an open shame.

Those who were partakers of the Holy Spirit and fell away were never truly converted though they were covenant members, and the Spirit was removed from them. Likewise in Hebrews 10:26 some in the covenant continued to sin willfully after receiving the knowledge of the truth, consequently "there no longer remains a sacrifice for sins." God's Spirit will not always strive with men, and even the Pharisees, covenant members while Jesus was physically present, were told that if they refused the working of the Holy Spirit, they had committed the unpardonable sin.

Jesus versus Satan

We should not say Jesus *versus* Satan as if the two are battling over the earth, for Jesus has already won and is reigning now. Dispensationalists postpone Jesus' reign to the so-called millennium, denying His regal realm now and giving it to Satan. If "Satan is alive and well on planet earth" in the sense that he rules the world, then antinomianism is established. How? Allegedly, obedience to God's laws does not bring success in the earth as Satan overrules God's children, and disobedience does not necessarily bring God's curse. Indeed, it is Satan and his seed that will conquer the earth by their wickedness and

---

[13]See Paul's covenantal fear in 1 Corinthians 9:27.

disobedience, not Jesus and His seed through the Gospel and obedience (contrary to Gen. 3:15; Rom. 16:20; 1 Cor. 15:22-26), further indicating that God's laws are irrelevant. In other words, the more antinomian Satan and his people become, the more success they will have in spreading wickedness and Satan's kingdom in the world, hastening the end of the world, rather than the biblical truth that disobedience reaps judgment, shrinking Satan's kingdom. Similarly, when carried over into salvation, the Christian who is antinomian, giving ultimate allegiance to Satan, will still go to heaven. Therefore, we have the incredible conclusion that wickedness is "blessed" and nothing is accomplished by obedience.[14]

Apparently dispensationalists have not understood that moral law is God's creation, being only One lawgiver (James 4:12), that man cannot create moral law, and that every law enacted by man is either an application of God's law or an act of rebellion, with neutrality being impossible (Isa. 8:19-20). Christ rules the world providentially by sovereign power but especially by His moral law, and those who obey are blessed and those who disobey are cursed. This is Jesus' world, not Satan's, and the terms are His.[15]

Conditional versus Unconditional Covenants

We should not say conditional *versus* unconditional covenants as if the two are separate, but dispensationalists only hold to the unconditional aspect. The Old Testament covenants were supposedly unconditional promises to Abraham and David that they would have the land of Palestine forever. It made no difference what Abraham and David did or if they had faith; the land was theirs forever.[16] This same idea is transferred to salvation so once one enters the covenant, it does

---

[14]Even in the so-called millennial reign, Jesus will not be successful.

[15]For more on Jesus ruling and not Satan, covering the passages pertinent to the issue, see my book, *Man as God: The Word of Faith Movement*, chapter 10, which may be ordered from the publisher in the front of this book.

[16]"Forever" is usually interpreted as 1000 years in the so-called millennium.

not matter what one does — the covenant is unconditional. Dispensationalists have never understood the Reformed and biblical idea that the covenants are both unconditional and conditional, depending on the point of view. From God's view, He knows His own, and it is certain they will arrive safely home (unconditional). From man's view, the promise is to those who persevere (conditional). God gives to His elect what He requires: the ability to persevere in faith and holiness. Likewise salvation (not just justification) is conditioned on a faith that perseveres, and Jesus gives faith to His elect and the Holy Spirit to enable them to persevere.[17] The very warnings in Scripture are used to keep the elect on the path of holiness and to cause the reprobate to manifest themselves. The law becomes a blessing to the elect as they love it and keep it (imperfectly) by the Spirit while the same law is a curse to the reprobate who hate it and crash on it, making havoc of their lives. Yet both could be in the covenant as historically manifested.

Dillow charges that to condition salvation on perseverance is to be Roman Catholic, suspending the final verdict of one's state until the end. He misunderstands the conditional/unconditional nature of the covenant of grace. Salvation (justification to glorification) is both conditional and unconditional. God promises heaven to those who will meet the condition of faith, but He gives faith to His elect unconditionally. Dillow believes that salvation is settled when the person believes, for at this point he has met the condition; but the Reformed believe that salvation is settled before the world began: "He chose us in Him before the foundation of the world" and that this choosing had certain moral consequences: "that we should be holy and without blame before Him in love" (Eph. 1:4). Dillow thinks that the sinner makes his salvation sure by his faith while the Reformed, reflecting Scripture, assert that God makes it sure. It is emphatically not true that the Reformed think that one's salvation is unsure *with God* until he perseveres to the end, though it may be so to himself and to others.

---

[17]We do not deny that justification is legal and accomplished at the instant one believes the Gospel and cannot be improved, but we only emphasize that the kind of faith that justifies is one that perseveres.

A Bible college professor once lamented that the brightest students of the dispensational college were abandoning dispensationalism for the Reformed faith, especially when they abandoned the dispensational concept of law and grace and of Pelagianism. The answer to his puzzle is obvious: Once one sees that salvation is all of grace (no Pelagianism), that in "the volume of the Book" it is written of Jesus, so that all saving faith is in Him, that law and grace imply one another, that there is only one way to be justified, then the logical conclusion is that Jesus is the Head of His *one* people as their legal representative. Hence there are not two brides or two peoples of God, and the Bible is seen as a book of unity rather than diversity.

Biblical Index

Subject & Personal Index